Small-Scale Evaluati

Small-Scale Evaluation in Health

A Practical Guide

Sinead Brophy, Helen Snooks and Lesley Griffiths

Los Angeles • London • New Delhi • Singapore

SAGE Publications Ltd
1 Oliver's Yard
55 City Road
London EC1Y 1SP

SAGE Publications Inc.
2455 Teller Road
Thousand Oaks, California 91320

SAGE Publications India Pvt Ltd
B 1/I 1 Mohan Cooperative Industrial Area
Mathura Road
New Delhi 110 044

SAGE Publications Asia-Pacific Pte Ltd
33 Pekin Street #02-01
Far East Square
Singapore 048763

Library of Congress Control Number: 2007931483

British Library Cataloguing in Publication data

A catalogue record for this book is available from the British Library

ISBN 978-1-4129-3006-2
ISBN 978-1-4129-3007-9 (pbk)

Typeset by C&M Digitals (P) Ltd., Chennai, India
Printed in Great Britain by The Cromwell Press Ltd, Trowbridge, Wiltshire
Printed on paper from sustainable resources

Contents

List of Figures

List of Case Studies

Acknowledgements

We would like to thank Professor Ceri Phillips for his help and advice in drafting the health economics components of the book; Mary Halter for providing invaluable comments; and Sopna Mannan and Michael Brophy for reading the book and providing feedback.

About this Book

This handbook takes a simple approach to evaluation, written for non-researchers with no previous experience of conducting evaluations. It is a simple-language handbook with a self-learning approach and is accompanied by five self-learning courses that the reader can work through to develop their skills further in the methods and analysis involved in evaluation. This book is a complete guide to simple evaluation with references and advice which guide access to further information, according to the individual reader's needs.

Author Biographies

Sinead Brophy is a senior lecturer in Epidemiology and Public Health at the Centre for Health Information and Research and Evaluation (CHIRAL) in the School of Medicine at Swansea University. She has worked in the field of epidemiology and management of chronic disease for 10 years and has an interest in the secondary use of data, such as using routinely collected data (hospital admissions, medical records) to examine management of chronic disease.

Helen Snooks is professor in Health Services Research, based in the Centre for Health Information Research and Evaluation (CHIRAL) in the School of Medicine at Swansea University. She is currently Director of AWARD's Mid and West Wales section. Her main research interests and expertise lie in the fields of emergency pre-hospital and immediate care, clinical audit and effectiveness, and research support. In these areas, the focus of her work is to plan, design and carry out evaluations of new models of service delivery, which often involves changing roles and working across boundaries between service providers. Her work is strongly patient-focused and collaborative, and uses mixed methods to achieve study aims. In recent years her research support work has taken her to new areas, and she has recently been involved in diverse studies concerning the evaluation of a national bibliotherapy scheme in Wales; NHS Direct Wales, the organisation of primary care nursing, the provision of gastrointestinal services and community action research.

Lesley Griffiths holds a personal chair at the University of Wales, Swansea. She is a sociologist who specialises in research which explores the experience of patients, service users and carers. She has a particular interest in the use of qualitative methods, especially in methods designed to analyse talk and text. She has a second role as Associate Director of Involving People/Cynnwys Pobl, the Welsh research infrastructure organisation funded to facilitate the involvement of patients, service users and carers as active partners in research.

Michael Brooks (illustrator) graduated with a degree in design from the University of Portsmouth in 1995 and is a freelance illustrator/graphic designer.

1 What is an Evaluation?

What is an evaluation?
What do we mean by small-scale evaluation?
Why evaluate?
What shapes an evaluation?
What evaluation can and cannot do?
Who should do the evaluation?
How do we do an evaluation?

OVERVIEW

What is an evaluation?

What is an evaluation?

Evaluation means to assess the value of something. This raises a very important question for any evaluation – valuable in terms of what? Why an evaluation is being done, and who it is being done for, will determine how it is carried out and what it aims to assess.

Results of evaluations are often used to make decisions about competing health care options. When we do an evaluation we are normally asking questions like 'does it work?' and 'is it worth it?'

Importantly, evaluation should be systematic in terms of assessment and reporting. It therefore needs to be carried out in a way that allows other people to follow the aims and methods and perhaps to repeat the evaluation themselves elsewhere. It should always be easy to see from the write-up of an evaluation how it was done, what information was collected and how it was analysed. Results should be provided as well as conclusions so that their validity (how believable they are) can be assessed.

What do we mean by small-scale evaluation?

Carrying out research can be time consuming and expensive. Evidence that is published about the clinical effectiveness of treatments or services is often produced through large-scale – usually multi-centre – studies that can cost hundreds of thousands of pounds to complete. In this book we aim to provide guidance for those who wish to undertake local, small-scale studies that will be run from within existing budgets, or with a modest amount set aside to carry out or commission an evaluation. It is important to recognise that, within these constraints, it is usually not possible to answer questions that require a complex study design, the recruitment of hundreds or even thousands of patients, and the sophisticated statistical or qualitative analysis of data. Questions concerning the clinical effectiveness of new treatments or services that include the assessment and comparison of health outcomes of patients (for example, measurement of symptoms; assessment of disability; assessment of quality of life) are unlikely to be answerable within small-scale, local, low budget evaluations. But there are important questions that service commissioners and planners do want to know about how new services are running, such as: are patients seen more quickly? Are staff happy with the new arrangements? Are sessions well attended? This book is designed to help practitioners and managers to plan and carry out evaluations of services that are relevant to their needs, and which will produce findings that are valid and can be relied upon for informing decision making.

In summary: Evaluation is a systematic assessment of the value of something. Understanding gained from an evaluation allows us to help plan a programme better, make improvements and inform decisions about whether a treatment or process should continue, and whether it should be more widely implemented.

Why evaluate?

Effects of treatments or services are not always predictable. Sometimes a service or treatment is introduced with the best possible intention but the consequences can actually result in people being worse off. For example, the introduction of fruit stalls in schools led to children eating less fruit (see Case Study 1.1). Evaluation can identify any negative impacts of services as well as the positive.

CASE STUDY 1.1

Evaluation of fruit stalls in four schools in South Wales

Background: In an initiative to encourage healthy eating, the local health board provided the equipment to develop fruit stalls in participating local schools. These stalls were set up as non-profit-making shops offering low-cost fruit and vegetable to children along with healthy snacks.

Methods: Stalls were implemented in stages, with two schools introducing stalls early on and two control schools introducing stalls at a later stage. Number of items of fruit eaten was compared by observation of the behaviour of randomly selected children (n = 40) in control and intervention schools.

Results: Before the intervention children in both the control and intervention school consumed on average 1.5 portions of fruit or vegetables per child during school time. After the intervention the control school children consumed an average of two portions and the intervention school children consumed an average of 0.5 portions per child (much of this was due to the intake of tomato sauce) [$p < 0.001$ Difference 1.5 (95 per cent CI: 1.01–1.99].

Observations of lunch box contents showed that parents in the control schools gave children fruit and juice. However, in the intervention schools, parents gave the children money to buy low-price fruit and no longer provided fruit and juice.

Conclusion: In the intervention schools, children chose to keep the money rather than buy fruit and were more likely to purchase non-health items such as crisps, chips and sweets. Therefore, fruit stalls in schools do not encourage fruit consumption, but schools that encourage parents to provide a healthy lunch and also to encourage a healthy lifestyle can influence total fruit and vegetable consumption during the school period. These findings are based on schools that already have a good record in healthy eating. Findings may differ in schools with a poor record in fruit consumption.

Source: hypothetical example

Question: What could we have done first which could have helped predict that fruit stalls would not work?

In addition, money for health care is in short supply. So that scarce resources are spent in a way that achieves benefits across communities, understanding is needed about the effects of innovations in treatments and services. We need to collect and report information about such effects as well as information about how the treatment or service is delivered. For example,

Competing health care options

we may wish to compare two different models of care (such as different types of anaesthesia, see Case Study 1.2) designed to deliver similar results in order to decide which is more acceptable to patients. This information can help to plan both local service delivery for the benefit of users, as well as potentially the wider population to inform larger-scale research for service and policy development.

Patients' self-evaluation after 4–12 weeks following propofol or xenon anaesthesia: a comparison

Aims: The evaluation set out to assess patients' self-assessment of the two types of anaesthesia after having an operation. The two types of anaesthesia evaluated were propofol (an injectable general anaesthetic) and xenon (gas anaesthetic).

Methods: The evaluation looked at 160 patients aged between 18 years to 60 years who were undergoing elective surgery. Patients were randomly given either an injected anaesthetic (propofol) or a gas anaesthetic (xenon). The patients were telephoned to ask for their assessment of the anaesthetic. The patients did not know which type of anaesthetic they received and the people conducting the interview did not know which type of anaesthetic the patient had received. Patients were asked about: their evaluation of the anaesthesia; choice of the same anaesthesia for the future; recall of uncomfortable feelings after the anaesthesia.

Findings: 116 took part in the telephone interview. The two study groups (that is, those taking injected, those taking gas anaesthesia) were comparable with respect to age, weight, height and gender. There was no difference between the groups in terms of self-evaluation of anaesthesia, taking the same anaesthesia again or recall of uncomfortable feelings. However, the post-operative pain and appetite/thirst were higher (worse) for those taking the gas (xenon) anaesthesia compared to those receiving the injected anaesthesia (propofol).

Source: Adapted from an abstract published by M. Coburn, O. Kunitz, J. Baumert, K. Hecker and R. Rossaint, *European Journal of Anaesthesiology*, 2005, 22 (11): 870–74.

Question: What conclusions can we come to using the results of this evaluation?

If services are not evaluated in a rigorous and systematic way, then we cannot be sure that resources are being used to best effect – some services may continue to be funded when they are ineffective, and others may not be implemented, or will be discontinued when they could achieve more. Basing decisions about how to use scarce resources only on the views of those delivering services may mean that those who are able to shout loudest – or those who have the most influential contacts – may be the most success-ful in attracting funding for their services. This cannot be the most rational way of spending money for the benefit of the whole community, and the decision-making processes are unlikely to be understandable or justifiable to people not directly involved. We can be much more confident about making the best possible decision if we know that our decision is based on evidence obtained from a rigorous and systematic evaluation.

Therefore, evaluations are carried out to make services more effective and justify decisions for funding in a transparent way.

What shapes an evaluation?

The aims of evaluation can vary depending on who it's being done for. Project funders often commission evaluation because they want to assess whether their money was used successfully. For example, funders might wish to evaluate an exercise programme in terms of effectiveness (see Case Study 1.3); they would therefore examine people who had done the exercise to see whether their fitness had improved (muscle strength and blood pressure). Who the evaluation is for is also very important for how the evaluation is carried out and what it is supposed to do. An evaluation can only provide the evidence it is set up to provide, and this relies on appropriate identification of objectives and methods to match. Evaluations rarely find anything useful if they have not been planned and designed properly.

Evaluation of a community-based exercise programme for elderly Korean immigrants

Aims: The evaluation set out to examine the feasibility and effectiveness of a modified exercise programme for elderly Korean immigrants (EKIs).

Methods: We recruited elderly Korean immigrants through posted fliers and with help from a Korean social worker. Participants in the exercise programme (n = 13) were elderly Korean people whose average age was 77 years, but ages ranged between 67–86 years. A Korean-American instructor taught a modified version of an evidence-based exercise programme three times weekly, 50 minutes per session, for 12 weeks.

The exercise programme was evaluated by examining exercise adherence (i.e. did the participants do the exercises?), measures of health before and after the exercise programme and satisfaction with the exercise programme. Group discussion was used to evaluate satisfaction with the exercise programme.

Findings: Participants showed improved muscle strength, agility/balance and blood pressure after the exercise programme.

(Continued)

CASE STUDY 1.3

(Continued)

All the participants were satisfied with the exercise programme, and participation rates were good (nine participants attended ≥ 80 per cent of classes).

Conclusions: The exercise programme was feasible for this sample and should be evaluated in a larger population of elderly Korean immigrants and in populations of other ethnic minorities.

Source: Adapted from M.K. Sin, B. Belza, J. Logerfo and S. Cunningham (2005) 'Evaluation of a Community-Based Exercise Programme for Elderly Korean Immigrants'. *Public Health Nursing*, 22 (5): 407–13.

Question: Why is this an evaluation and not an audit?

Appropriate evaluation can allow us explicitly to include the views of everyone involved in a treatment or programme, such as patients, service users, carers and health care workers as well as managers and policy makers. People from these different groups are likely to have different priorities and perspectives about what the most important effects of a service or treatment might be. This is especially relevant, for example, to the re-location and centralisation of services. Without a well planned and appropriately designed evaluation, it is unlikely that this range of views will be reported.

Therefore, the questions asked in an evaluation are shaped by who wants the evaluation done (who is funding it) and who is going to use the results and findings in the end.

What evaluation can and cannot do

Evaluation can give a clear answer to a specific question. However, evaluation cannot ask every possible question and provide every possible answer. The questions asked and the answers sought must be clearly planned and defined from the beginning. For example, unpredictable effects are unlikely to be identified unless methods are explicitly included to ensure they are picked up.

Evaluation can explore whether programme targets, or aims, are met and provides evidence to inform decision making. However, it cannot look at everything a programme might do. For example, we might wish to find out through evaluation whether nurse-led telephone helplines reduce call-out of emergency ambulances. We might find out that they do not, and this could be seen by some as a failure of the service. However, if we evaluated use of the helpline in terms of users' self-confidence to deal with their condition themselves, we might find it is a great success in these terms.

Most evaluations ask questions like 'Does it work?' but not necessarily 'How or why does it work?' These questions can be specifically built into an evaluation, but are not essential to all evaluations – if this understanding is required it needs to be identified at the outset so that appropriate objectives and methods can be defined, planned and incorporated into the evaluation. Questions like how and why something works, which involve describing the ways in which services or treatments are delivered, may require more complex approaches and methods. Sometimes evaluations are carried out to gather information about impact, with the assumption that an understanding of how and why the effects have happened will be gained as an automatic outcome of the study. It is important to recognise that this understanding is unlikely to be gained unless methods designed to capture this information are included. An evaluation may focus on the weaknesses of a system in order to investigate how to improve these areas. For example, interviewing people who do not attend regular screening tests for cervical cancer could help to highlight how the system could be made more accessible.

Understanding of how

It is important to recognise the limitations of small-scale evaluation of an established service. For instance, in an evaluation of a diabetes educational programme it would be very difficult to show that people on the programme have fewer eye problems or kidney complications, and even harder to demonstrate that the programme has led to any improvements in health. So, alternative or 'proxy' measures could be selected, such as attendance rates or changes in people's health-related behaviour (exercise levels, diet changes), or people's views about the programme could be gathered through interviews or focus groups.

Who should do the evaluation?

Many experts recommend that the evaluation of a programme or treatment should be carried out by a person who is independent, as this will make it more likely that they are not biased. If a person's job depends on a treatment working, then they may be more inclined to show the beneficial effects of the treatment and their findings may not be accurate or unbiased. This approach requires the person doing the evaluation to be 'neutral'. However, in order to understand the effects of a treatment or programme, it may be important to involve those people who provide and use the service at the planning stages of the evaluation. They will be the ones who will understand what aspects are important enough to include in the evaluation and the best way to incorporate the gathering of data alongside treatment delivery. Therefore, for successful evaluation, it is important to involve those who are giving and receiving the treatment. Indeed, in some forms of research, for example action research, the active participation of people involved in service delivery as well as service users is fundamental to the evaluation process.

It is important to make efforts to avoid any bias creeping in whilst the evaluation is underway, for example, in data collection or analysis. This can be

done, for instance, by keeping records of those who are not invited to participate as well as any patients recruited to the study, or by 'blinding' or keeping information hidden from the person carrying out the analysis which identifies patients and whether or not they had received the new service. This will help to ensure that biases are minimised. This need not mean that stakeholders, such as service providers and users, are kept out of the process of interpreting results. This is normally encouraged as good practice.

In summary: A good evaluation should be systematic, rigorous, and written up fully, so that others can see how the evaluation was carried out and that the conclusions drawn are based only on the results reported.

How do we do an evaluation?

The steps are:

- Develop a clear idea of what question we are asking.
- Examine what other people have done in this area.
- Form a plan of what we would like to do .
- Do a trial run of what we intend to do (a pilot to identify any problems).
- Collect all the data.
- Analyse the data.
- Write a report that includes objectives, methods, results, interpretation and recommendations.

Summary

- Evaluation assesses the value of something.
- It can be used to: see what has been achieved; identify the strengths and weakness of a system; compare the effects of a programme with other similar programmes; share experiences with others; assess whether the cost of something is worth the benefits it gives; make something more effective; help plan for the future.
- WHY you want to do an evaluation will determine HOW you do the evaluation.
- Good evaluation is systematic and rigorous, with methods and results described in full, and the conclusions drawn should be supported by evidence from the results of the evaluation.
- It is vital to recognise from the outset that any evaluation will only provide answers to questions which are clearly defined and addressed in the project. This means that unless evaluations have clearly identified aims and goals which are matched with appropriate methods, they are unlikely to succeed.

Frequently asked questions

What is the difference between research, evaluation and a clinical audit?

Research in health care is enquiry designed to produce new knowledge that can be applied more generally than in the setting in which it took place. The term can be used quite widely, and covers all types of approaches – including randomised controlled trials; exploratory enquiry; work to develop methods; and participative, action research.

Evaluation is a type of research, and examines the evidence to help decide what is best practice. Evaluation research always assesses the value of something, often in terms of costs and benefits.

A clinical audit examines whether treatments or services are being delivered to patients according to best practice. In auditing we are comparing what we are doing against an agreed – and usually evidence-based – standard.

In an audit, patients are not asked to have or do anything beyond the normal clinical care. However, in an evaluation (and research) we may ask patients to take or do things that are new and are not within normal clinical practice in order to examine the effect of these new treatments or procedures.

For more information see: www.geh-tr.wmichs.nhs.uk/services/orthopaedics/Audit%20and%20research/auditvsresearchleaflet.pdf and also www.btuheks.nhs./uk/cg/difference-audit-research.pdf

Importantly, we normally need to gain ethical approval from a Research Ethics Committee before carrying out any research study in a health care setting. By contrast, clinical audit is seen as a fundamental part of the delivery of health care, for which ethical approval is not required. The carrying out of evaluation can require ethical approval, although it can be viewed as part of service delivery, depending on its aims and methods. More guidance about whether we need to apply for ethical approval for a proposed study can be found at www.nres.npsa.nhs.uk/docs/guidance/Is_and_As_Differentiating_Research.pdf

Should we evaluate our own programme or commission others to do this?

We can choose to do either – or a bit of both. In designing the evaluation there should be input from the people involved in delivering the programme and those involved in the programme. However, in conducting the evaluation (e.g. doing interviews, recording the results) the 'researcher' should be independent of the programme, unless an action research approach is explicitly taken. The interpretation should be based on the findings of the independent researcher being put into context together with discussions with the people involved in receiving and delivering the programme.

The important thing is to recognise the strengths and weaknesses of each approach, and decide what suits us best, considering the resources, skills and time that are available for our proposed evaluation.

We're not sure about how to evaluate our programme; isn't it best to collect and store a wide range of data and then work out our evaluation plan later?

No, if you aren't clear about what you want to evaluate, how will you know what to collect? You might not collect something important, and will certainly collect huge reams of things you will never need. This is a great waste of resources and both your own and the participants' time. Conducting an evaluation like this will almost certainly lead you to not being able to answer your questions properly.

Further reading

Marie-Therese Feuerstein (1997) *Partners in Evaluation: Evaluating development and community programmes with participants*. London: Macmillan Education.

David Grembowski (2001) *The Practice of Health Program Evaluation*. London: Sage.

Ray Pawson and Nick Tilley (1997) *Realistic Evaluation*. London: Sage.

Colin Robson (2000) *Small Scale Evaluations: Principles and practice*. London: Sage.

Web pages
www.elwa.org.uk/elwaweb/elwa.aspx?pageid=2065
www.emro.who.int/rpc/pdf/healthresearchers_guide.pdf

2 Searching and Reviewing the Literature

Why do a search of the literature?

It is important to look at work other people have done and so set the evaluation in context. We undertake some background reading to help:

- understand how our evaluation fits in with the evidence already available around the topic
- design and plan the evaluation with the knowledge of what methods have worked or not worked for other people
- explain to others the reasons for doing this evaluation
- make sense of our findings against the backdrop of other people's work.

For example, we might be investigating the opinion of patients regarding a clinic (Case Study 2.1). We might do some background reading to:

- see how other people have undertaken this type of evaluation. We can look at published papers and government reports to examine and compare other people's methods of seeking patient's opinions regarding clinics.
- develop a better understanding of the main issues that are important to patients when they attend a clinic. Understanding the problem means we can make sure we ask the right questions and collect the right data. For example, other research might have examined waiting times, cleanliness, privacy – are these issues we should examine in our evaluation?

- explain why the evaluation needs to be done and demonstrate that there is a problem that needs addressing.
- help understand what our findings mean in relation to existing work.

CASE STUDY 2.1

The evaluation of family planning services in a mother-and-child centre

Objectives: To examine the views of women regarding the service provided at a mother-and-child family planning clinic.

Methods: All women attending the clinic between March 2005 and June 2005 were asked to complete an anonymous questionnaire. Women who could not complete the questionnaire were invited to participate in a structured interview. This descriptive, cross-sectional study obtained the views of 235 women out of 360 (65 per cent) attending the clinic.

Results: Women reported a high level of satisfaction (95 per cent were very satisfied with their visit). The most important aspects of the clinic for women were rated as (1) approachability of staff, (2) speed of receiving treatment/contraceptive interventions, (3) hygienic conditions. The majority of women (89 per cent) felt the hygienic conditions were excellent and staff were professional (92 per cent) and approachable (96 per cent). However, only 52 per cent of women felt the length of time spent waiting to receive their contraception (median time one week) was acceptable. Women in general (90 per cent) would have preferred to receive treatment/contraception intervention on the day of attendance. However, currently the clinic is nurse led and prescriptions cannot be given on the same day as attendance.

Conclusions: The clinic performs well in terms of hygiene and quality of care by the staff. However, time to treatment is thought to be too long for many women. A recommendation for the future would be to have a doctor in the clinic to prescribe contraceptive treatment.

Source: hypothetical example

Question: There is no background given to the topic in this abstract. What would you have liked to know in terms of background?

In summary: Background reading should be carried out throughout the evaluation as it helps us to plan our approach to the evaluation, and to benefit from the work that others have already carried out in the area. It also ensures that any findings have the best chance of being useful as they build on other peoples' work.

What does searching the literature involve?

1. Thinking about the topic we want to examine and planning how we will carry out a search of the literature related to our topic.
2. Formulating the places to look.
3. Doing the search.
4. Examining the results we get from the search.
5. Feeding the search findings into the evaluation plan and its execution.

Thinking about the topic

What are we searching for?   We need to think about what we want to find out and consider what words would best describe the topic that can also be used as search terms. For example, if we are interested in looking at the use of a computerised prescription system to reduce prescribing errors, we would want to look up articles that contained the words 'prescribing errors', 'computerised prescription system' or 'computerized prescription system' (see Case Study 2.2).

Medical errors in an internal medicine department: evaluation of a computerised prescription system

CASE STUDY 2.2

Background: Medication errors include errors in dosing, transcribing and dispensing medications. They can result in serious patient morbidity and mortality. Analysis has shown that prevention strategies that reinforce systems instead of targeting individuals are the most effective. Computerised physician order entry (CPOE) is an intervention that targets the ordering stage of medications. Herein we examine CPOE in an internal medicine department in order to examine the level of error that occurs with this system.

Method: The study was carried out from December 2001 to January 2002. After two years of using the CPOE system, medication errors were evaluated prospectively in the internal medical department of a 360-bed academic hospital. Pharmacists reviewed all medical records and compared them with the entries on the CPOE system. Medical errors detected were recorded on a data collection form with a design based on the types of errors as defined by the American Society of Hospital Pharmacists (ASHP). Completed forms were reviewed and medication errors were classed according to ASHP Guidelines.

(Continued)

(Continued)

Results: A total of 2268 prescriptions were monitored (162 patients). In these prescriptions, 73 medical errors (22.4 per cent of the patients) were detected (59 prescribing errors and 14 monitoring errors). The most common prescribing errors were deficiencies related to the right class but the wrong drug (28.3 per cent), incorrect dose (30 per cent) and unclear orders (13.3 per cent). Errors related to the incorrect frequency of administration (5 per cent), the maintenance of an IV route (5 per cent) and duplicated drug therapy (11.7 per cent). Drug interactions (1.7 per cent) and length of therapy (3.3 per cent) were also detected. The 14 monitoring errors detected were failures to review a prescribed regimen for appropriateness and the detection of problems.

Conclusion: The CPOE system is open to errors. The main type of error is a prescribing error of the wrong dose or the wrong type but the right class of drug. These are potentially serious errors and therefore a second double-checking mechanism is needed when implementing the CPOE system.

Source: Adapted from A. Mirco et al., *Pharmaceutical World Science* (2005) 27: 351–2.

Question: What do you think of this background, and what else could the authors have added?

How will we carry out the literature search?   One of the most challenging aspects of searching effectively for relevant literature is ensuring that the search is properly focused. Searches can be focused in several ways: by topic, by language, by geographical location of studies, by date of publication (for example, only studies published within the last two years), and by type of article (for example, reviews only, reports of trials only and so on).

Where are we going to look?   Before starting a search it is much easier if you are a member of a library at a university or hospital. If you do not already have access to an academic library through your work, it would be useful to see if you can go to a local hospital or university library to use their facilities. Librarians have a great deal of experience in searching for and accessing materials and may be able to help you. There are many sources of background material that we may wish to use to inform our evaluation. We could include only published academic work, that is, articles in peer reviewed journals, or extend the search to include unpublished reports (so-called grey literature), or even go so far as to contacting specialists in the field.

Places to look

- It is usually best to start by reading recent general reviews or commentaries which will provide us with an overview of the topic. These will often provide signposts to other relevant material. It is important to be clear that for small-scale evaluations we are not attempting to carry out a full systematic review of the topic area as this would be a project in its own right. Rather, we want to ensure that key findings from previous work are identified and used to inform our evaluation.
- To find reviews and examine published articles in relevant journals, we will need to look up some databases which hold these journal articles. For example, Pubmed (Medline) is available at www.pubmed.gov and is free to access and use. The Cochrane Collaboration holds details of papers which are systematic reviews or summaries of all the randomised controlled trials that have been carried out on a topic, as well as other types of research. This is also free to access for most people at www.the cochranelibrary.com. Some others that can be accessed using a university or hospital library are Web of Knowledge, EMBASE (Excerpta Medica database), the British Nursing Index or CINAHL (Cumulative Index to Nursing and Allied Health). These databases are also available in some larger public libraries on CD-ROM.
- Once we have retrieved our first set of papers from the search, it can be very helpful to read through the reference lists provided at the end of each paper to identify further papers or check that we have retrieved all the relevant work.
- If we are going to refer to a recent news item, many articles are now available online over the Internet, for example, newspaper sites or the BBC's website.
- The Internet can be a quick and easy additional way to search for information. However, we do always need to make sure that the source on the web is reliable, as anyone can publish anything on the Internet. One place that is useful to start a search is Google Scholar (http://scholar. google.com/).
- Organisations which are active in the field of interest and identified through the literature search can always be contacted with a request for additional information and a list of their publications and reports.
- Another useful method for identifying relevant papers on a focused topic is to browse the specialist journals for the area – sometimes referred to as 'hand-searching'.
- We might talk to other people in the field and perhaps contact specialists in the area to get their recommendations for books and papers. We may also identify key researchers who have published widely on a topic and contact them.

Doing the search

When we have established the topic we want to search for, we can start to put together the words we want to use into a search strategy. New users of

Medline/Pubmed can benefit from seeking the advice of a librarian as well as using the tutorials provided with Pubmed (see the left-hand side of the screen). These only take a few minutes to run and are very helpful in getting started.

There are some terms used across databases which are helpful in carrying out searches. These include AND, OR and NOT. These are often called Boolean operators and normally have to be written in capital letters. They can be used to do Internet searches as well as searches of databases containing research articles. Some basic terms to use in a search strategy are listed below, followed by more tips.

AND: If we want to put together two words so that any articles have to contain both words, we can use the word AND (in capital letters). So a search of 'heart attack AND aspirin' would give any article that deals with both heart attack and aspirin. Any paper that dealt with only one of these would be excluded from the results of this search.

OR: If the condition we are searching for has more than one name or spelling we can use OR, for example, 'heart attack OR myocardial infarction', 'computerised prescription system OR computerised prescription system'.

( ):   We can combine the two terms described above by using brackets. For example, to identify papers that include a range of different terms or spellings which refer to heart attacks but also refer to aspirin, we can type '(heart attack OR myocardial infarction)' AND aspirin. This means any articles that deal with both heart attack and aspirin or both myocardial infarction and aspirin will be returned.

NOT: If we want to exclude some types or groups of people or treatments, for example, only articles on adults, then we can specify NOT in the search: (heart attack OR myocardial infarction) AND aspirin NOT (child OR paediatric OR infant).

[AU]:   If we want to search for a specific author, we can type the author's name followed by [AU], and articles with that author's name will be returned. For example, Brown M. will bring up a lot of articles containing the word Brown, but Brown M. [AU] will only give articles where M. Brown is an author.

[TI]:   If we want to search for articles with a certain word in the title, we can use [TI]. Therefore 'myocardial infarction [TI]' will only give articles with myocardial infarction in the title.

[TW]:   If we want to search for a word in the title or abstract we can type [TW], which means text word. This means articles with an author who has this word as their surname will not be found. For example, 'coffee' may be the topic we would like to look up but there are a number of articles where the author has a surname of Coffee, which we will want to exclude.

Sometimes initial searches can be quite overwhelming as they may return far more material than it seems possible to read. In these circumstances we can limit the search in various ways so that the project is manageable and focused. For example:

- We can select the 'Limits' button in Pubmed. With this menu we can limit the time period we want to search. For example, we can put in the exact dates we want to search (that is, Jan 1990–Dec 2006), or search the most recent articles (Entrez date, which means date entered).
- We can limit our search to humans only, excluding all articles on animals, for example in laboratory studies (or vice versa).
- We can limit the search to articles about women only (or men only) if we are only interested in results from one sex.
- We can use truncation, which is to put part of the word followed by an asterisk to get all the variations of this word. For example, if we put 'hospital*' we could get all the articles about: hospital, hospitals, hospitalisation etc.

If in doubt about the search, always ask the help of a librarian.

When doing a search we must always keep a record of the search terms that we have used. This prevents us wasting time later on, and allows us to report – and others to see - how we have done our search and selected our references. We make a note of the web addresses of sites found, the name of the book and pages of interest, the names of journals and titles of articles that are of interest. This way if we want to quote or refer to any of the information we have found, it will be easy to locate the relevant source.

Examining the results of the search

Carrying out a literature search requires more than one session at the library or online. Following our initial searches, we always go through a process of revising and refining further searches. The first thing to do is to look at how many papers the search has identified. As we explained earlier, we may need to limit our searches in order to arrive at a feasible number of articles for us to examine.

The second step is to read the titles and abstracts to decide whether the article relates to the topic of interest, in which case we will want to retrieve the full paper.

Third, the studies that do relate to the topic of interest will need to be obtained from the journal in which they were published. If we are searching through a library at a university or hospital, often they will subscribe to the journals so we can just double-click on the link and will be taken directly to the article, or can retrieve a copy from the shelf. Sometimes we can pay for a specific article over the Internet, and sometimes we will need to order it through a library.

Keep a record of all the searches

Hierarchy of evidence

Of course, we then have to read all the papers we have retrieved. When reading the articles we will need to think about the strength of the evidence presented in each. In health research there is a system of rating the level of evidence provided according to the study design. This is called the hierarchy of evidence (Figure 2.1). For example, a letter from a hospital saying that they use a computer prescription system, and reporting that it is effective, is useful but not strong evidence. A systematic review, which combined the results of ten studies and showed a 35 per cent reduction in prescribing errors after the introduction of a computer prescription system, is very strong evidence. Of course different research methods that may not be rated highly by the hierarchy of evidence can still provide useful information about a particular topic. For example, qualitative research about the ways in which people have used or not used a computerised system could be very helpful in designing and implementing a system in a real-life situation.

Feeding the search findings into the evaluation plan

The articles we find can help us better understand the topic we are going to evaluate and help to plan what we are going to do in the evaluation. When we write the plan for the evaluation or the background section for the report, we will need to write a summary of the background reading to explain where the evaluation fits in the context of other peoples' work. When writing a background section we should not try to include every interesting thing we have read, but instead should try to identify the main points we want to make in relation to our evaluation objectives from our reading and then use the literature to substantiate these points. For example, if we are evaluating a computerised prescription system we might want to talk about prescription errors, what they are, what implications they have and why they are more common nowadays with more drugs and more contraindications to take into account. We might want to talk about different systems to overcome these errors, such as a computerised system, and give some history about the development and evaluation of the system by other people. However, we would need to keep our study focused on our objectives at all times. We would then use the background reading to reference the points we are making and back up our argument with evidence.

We should only select information that is directly relevant to a specific point we wish to make, as we would want to give an overview of the topic, focusing on key points and the main themes. The summary should try to show:

- what the topic is about
- what has been done in this field so far
- what the main issues are
- what we will do in light of the main issues
- what has already been done.

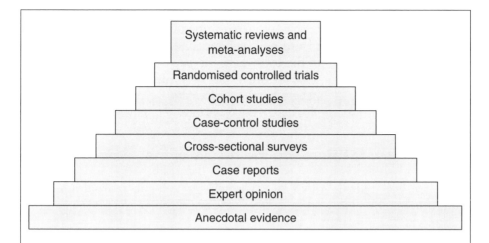

Anecdotal evidence – someone told you something works, or doesn't work.

Expert opinion – an editorial or a panel of experts draws up guidelines or gives a view of something based on many cases.

A case report – a systematic report using one example. It may be one hospital's experiences of a new system or one patient followed up after a new procedure.

Cross-sectional survey – a survey at one point in time.

Case control – people who have a disease as compared to people who do not have a disease in terms of things that might affect the disease. For example, people who have a stomach ulcer might take more anti-inflammatory tablets than people who do not have a stomach ulcer.

Cohort – Taking a group of people (the name comes from a cohort of Roman soldiers) and following them to see who develops the condition of interest. This is used for studies in work places where everyone in a certain job is followed but only some people may develop a disease. For example, those exposed to long-term noise may develop deafness. It could also be used to follow people with diabetes, some of whom attend a course and some who do not, and to see if control of the diabetes improves in those who attend a course. The important aspect of this study is that people should not have developed the condition or disease you are studying (e.g. deafness or improved control of diabetes) when the study starts.

Randomised controlled trial – assigning people to either receive a drug or attend a course (or any other intervention) in a random way (not dependent on, for example. the severity of their disease, the background of patients or the researcher's choice). This way those people who receive the drug and those who do not should be similar in everything except whether they are administrered the drug (that is, the same number of men and women, severe and mild disease, etc. in both groups).

A systematic review takes the results of completed studies – usually randomised controlled trials – and combines their results to give one overall answer.

A meta-analysis is the name for the statistical technique used to combine the findings of different studies on the same topic to give one overall, summary answer.

Figure 2.1   Hierarchy of evidence

 In order to properly report all the papers which have been referred to during the evaluation, it is necessary to provide a reference list which is linked to the points in the text where the papers are mentioned. This is done in order that any reader is able to find the papers for themselves and so read further, and can also assess the ways in which they have been used.

How to reference the results of the search

There are two main methods of referencing articles in journal and book publications. These are known as the Harvard (author-date) and Vancouver (author-number) reference systems.

Harvard (author-date) style

This system uses the author's name and date of publication in the body of the text, and the reference list is given alphabetically by author. For example: 'Medication errors are errors in the process of ordering, transcribing, dispensing or monitoring medication' (Kaushal, 2003). Names and dates are enclosed in brackets unless the author's name is part of the sentence.

If two papers are cited by the same author, and both are published in the same year, the first should be referenced as (Kaushal, 2003a), then (Kaushal, 2003b) and so on.

The full reference is listed at the end of the article, which is arranged in alphabetical order by author. Journal names are given in full and are italicised, as are book names. References would be cited as follows:

Bobb, A., Gleason, K., Husch, M., Feinglass, J., Yarnold, R.R. and Noskin, G.A. (2004), The epidemiology of prescribing errors. The potential impact of computerized prescriber order entry. *Archives of Internal Medicine*, vol. 164, pp. 785–92.

Carmenates, J. (2001), Impact of automation on pharmacist interventions and medication errors in a correction health care system. Yale University Press, London.

Kasushal, R., Shojania, K.G. and Bates, D.W. (2003), Effects of computerized physician order entry and clinical decision support systems on medication safety. A systematic review. *Archives of Internal Medicine* 2003; 163: 1409–16.

Vancouver (author-number) style

The Vancouver system uses numbers to indicate references. The list of references at the end of the document is then ordered by number as they appear in the text. For example:

Medication errors are errors in the process of ordering, transcribing, dispensing or monitoring medications [1]. The computerised physician order entry (CPOE) is a promising intervention that targets the ordering stage of medications, where most medication errors occur [1–3].

1.   Kaushal, R., Shojania, K.G. and Bates, D.W. Effects of computerized physician order entry and clinical decisions support systems on medication safety. A systematic review. *Arch Intern Med* 2003; 163: 1409–16.

2. American Society of Hospital Pharmacists. ASHP guidelines on preventing medication errors in hospitals. *Am J Hosp Pharm* 1993; 50: 3.5–14.
3. Bobb, A., Gleason, K. et al. The epidemiology of prescribing errors. The potential impact of computerized prescriber order entry. *Arch Intern Med* 2004; 164: 339–40.

Some readers find that the main text reads more easily using the Vancouver system, with each reference in the list uniquely related to a number, saving the reader time in searching alphabetically for the first author of a reference. However, the Harvard style is probably easier to manage as the order of papers remains alphabetical by author. The Vancouver style can be quite challenging, as the numbers in the text and in the reference list need to match exactly. When new references are added during revisions to the text, all the numbers need to be changed to reflect the added references. This can be done using a word-processing package, or software specially designed for this purpose such as Reference Manager or Endnote, or manually for short documents.

If our work is to be published, we must always check which style is acceptable to the publisher.

Summary

- Background reading allows us to put the evaluation into context and explain why we are doing the evaluation; it also helps us to interpret our results.
- To do background reading we need to decide the words that describe the topic of interest, the sources of information and how we will obtain the relevant references (that is, journals and books).
- We need to keep a record of all the searches so we know how to find references again.
- We should only use references to provide an evidence base for specific points we want to make in the background section and should not try to cover everything we may have read .

Frequently asked questions

I'm only interested in the effects of what is happening locally when we implement our changes – is it necessary for me to do any background reading?

Yes, background reading can help you to see the best methods of examining the changes you are implementing. We can also learn from what other people have done. Gaining a bit of background can help us interpret our findings and understand what has happened when we implemented our changes. The changes may be local but the methods and interpretation will always be something that we can learn from others and may be generalisable.

How do I know when I have identified enough of the relevant literature?

This can happen when you cannot finding anything new or anything you haven't heard of before even the reference lists of will papers – all refer to papers of which you are already aware. Sometimes it can just be that you have had all your specific questions answered, such as what did other people find when they brought in this new treatment? If we read a number of other articles which tell us what other people have found, we should have our answers. We don't need to read every paper ever written that discusses the new treatment, just enough to be satisfied that we have answered our questions.

How do I decide what material I should include?

We have to be very selective here and not end up writing an essay on the subject on which we did background reading. We will have done our reading to answer specific questions and thus we need to summarise just the answers to these questions. We must include the material that directly answers the questions we asked, and not go off on tangents regarding other things we have read that were interesting to us. Basically, we need to focus on the material that answers our specific, preset questions.

Where can I get advice about searching the literature?

The best place is your public library, or the library at a hospital, university etc. There are many help pages on journal databases and there is help on searching the web on the web itself. Quite a few university library websites have advice on doing literature searches, for example:

www2.plymouth.ac.uk/millbrook/rsources/sealit/srchguid.htm#Journal at Plymouth.

www.uwe.ac.uk/library/resources/econ/pdf/litsrch03.pdf at the University of West England.

How do I know which papers are the best quality?

We need to read papers with a critical eye. The hierarchy of evidence (see p. 19) gives us some advice on this, and the book recommended below by Trisha Greenhalgh gives a very detailed method for appraising the quality of papers. However, generally, if you think about what the paper says and what methods were used to carry out the study, and then think logically about any errors or problems or reasons why you may or may not believe the findings, this is really what critical appraisal is all about. In Chapter 3 we discuss validity and reliability, which are involved in assessing the quality of papers.

Further reading

Trisha Greenhalgh (2001) *How to Read a Paper: The basics of evidence based medicine.* London: BMJ Books.

J.A. Muir Gray (1997) *Evidence-based Healthcare: How to make health policy and management decisions.* London: Churchill Livingston.

Web pages

Literature searches:
www.shef.ac.uk/library/libdocs/ml-rs17.html
www.shef.ac.uk/scharr/ir/litsrch.html
http://admin.csp.org.uk/admin2/uploads/18bf072-f1f3bfb74e–7f1f/csp_litsearch_userguide.pdf
www.rgu.ac.uk/library/howto/page.cfm?pge=25989

Appraising literature:
www.shef.ac.uk/scharr/ir/units/critapp/appres.htm
www.phru.nhs.uk/casp/critical_appraisal_tools.htm
http://library.kent.ac.uk/library/info/subjectg/healthinfo/critapprais.shtml

3 Evaluation Design

Purpose of the evaluation
Evaluating from within?
Types of evaluations – what are we trying to find out?
Evaluation methods
Issues to consider when designing the evaluation

OVERVIEW

Evaluation design means the approach of the evaluation and is determined by the purpose and aims. Evaluation design is a description of the methods used. These methods will be influenced by issues such as what type of data and how much we need to collect.

Purpose of the evaluation

If the evaluation is to be fit for purpose it is important that this is taken account of when deciding on the design. For example, evaluations might be carried out to:

- establish how well something is working
- decide whether to continue with an intervention
- decide whether to extend or introduce an additional intervention
- find out whether money has been well spent on the intervention
- add to what is known about how an intervention works – how effective it is; how much it costs; how it works for certain groups of people (for example, the elderly and minority ethnic groups); how the intervention is delivered in real-life settings and so on.

These different purposes influence the way we carry out our evaluation – the type of design that is selected. For example, if we are carrying out an evaluation in order to establish whether to continue with or withdraw an intervention, we need to be clear about what sort of evidence we would need to make this decision so that we can use an appropriate design for our evaluation. What would be the key factor in deciding whether to continue a service – patient satisfaction? Health outcomes? Cost? Operational indicators? Or a combination of these? We cannot advise about these across studies – this needs to be decided for each evaluation that we undertake, in consultation with stakeholders.

The design – or approach – used for an evaluation depends on the questions that it aims to answer, but another major consideration in selecting the design is what resources are available to carry out the evaluation. It is easy to underestimate the costs, and quite often projects are expected to produce some sort of evaluation without money or other resources directly set aside to do this. It is important to remember that some evaluation designs are much more costly than others in terms of time, financial resources and expertise required. The evaluation needs to be set up with a design – and evaluation – objective that can be met within the resources available. It is important to know and understand the different ways in which evaluation can be undertaken, so that we:

- can choose the best evaluation design to answer our questions
- can plan our methods of data collection
- can understand what data we need to collect
- can see how other people have conducted this type of evaluation and learn from their experiences
- can comprehend the strengths and weaknesses of the evaluation design that we select: what questions the design can – and cannot – answer.

In ideal circumstances an evaluation strategy is built into programmes when they are designed. This allows for the collection of information about how things are before the programme starts (base line data), which then provides a very valuable comparison with the way things change as a result of the programme. It may also allow evaluators to plan key aspects of implementation with the service providers to allow effective evaluation, for example, introduction of the service in one area only, or on random days/weeks so that a comparator (control) group can be identified; or the development of routine data collection tools which include data items that will be relevant to the evaluation.

Evaluating from within?

The evaluation design and methods have to match exactly the questions we wish to answer through the evaluation. Evaluations can be carried out either internally (by people who are part of the organisation which is providing or participating in the intervention) or externally (by people from outside the organisation, who are employed specifically to undertake evaluations). Both approaches can have advantages and disadvantages.

Evaluating from within?

Internal evaluations have the advantage that evaluators generally understand the processes and people involved very well, and are therefore more likely to set up achievable targets for data collection. Of course this can also be a disadvantage, as it may be very difficult to remain objective if we find ourselves in a situation where people we know well will be adversely affected or dismayed by information we discover during our evaluation.

External evaluations will almost invariably be more expensive than internal evaluations, although the evaluators should not experience the same difficulties in remaining objective. External evaluators may be able to be more clear-headed and pursue evaluation goals without being influenced by personal relationships. However, data may be more difficult to access, and can be misinterpreted by 'outsiders' unless care is taken to ensure that they are kept well informed throughout the process. It is also possible to consider a design with outside data collection and inside evaluation.

Evaluations can be set up to involve all those with an interest in whether – and how – a service is delivered. As a general rule, all high-quality evaluations should include the views and perspectives of stakeholders (people affected by the evaluation) so that the right questions are asked, and to ensure that the data gathered are meaningful. This will also ensure that the findings are not rejected by a key stakeholder. But in some evaluations, the principle of involvement is taken further, so that stakeholders, including service users, practitioners and managers, sit alongside the evaluators from the outset of the evaluation, and each contributes their expertise and views throughout the study, in an equal way. This is generally called 'participatory evaluation', and 'action research' may be the approach used.

Types of evaluation – what are we trying to find out?

Evaluations may be designed to find out:

1. **Whether a programme or intervention is effective** – to feed into future funding decisions or for evidence to be used more widely. This is usually called a *summative evaluation* or *outcomes evaluation*. This is because it is designed to capture the impact of an intervention. In this type of evaluation we are measuring outcomes, for example, was whole body vibration reduced (see Case Study 3.1)? The data collected will give evidence related to this change. Quite often this type of evaluation is carried out by an external team, who are able to bring some detachment to the study – they are unlikely to be affected directly by the outcome of the study and may therefore be more able to plan, collect and interpret data without bias. Care must be taken in this type of evaluation to ensure that enough patients/service users are included in the sample to pick up an impact that is judged to be important. Objectives, outcomes and sample sizes must be carefully matched to avoid setting up a study that is too small to detect important differences in the measures selected. Generally we should seek the advice of a statistician to calculate the sample size that is needed.

Outcomes Evaluation: Evaluation of an occupational health intervention programme on whole-body vibration in fork-lift truck drivers: a controlled trial

Objectives: To evaluate the outcome of a multifaceted occupational health intervention programme on whole–body vibration (WBV) in fork-lift truck drivers.

Methods: We used an experimental study examining whole–body vibration pre-intervention and again post-intervention in both the experimental and control group. Occupational health services (OHS) delivered an intervention programme to the experimental group and delivered care as usual to the control group. In total, 15 OHSs, 32 OHS professionals, 26 companies and 260 fork-lift truck drivers were involved. Post-test measurements were carried out one year after the start of the programme.

Results: Before the intervention, baseline data showed no difference between experimental and control groups in terms of exposure to WBV. After the intervention there was a slight, even though not statistically significant, reduction of WBV exposure in the experimental group ($p=0.06$). This limited effect of the programme might be caused by the short period of follow-up and dropout amongst participants. The feasibility and the usefulness of the programme within the OHS setting were rated good by the participants.

Conclusion: The programme to decrease WBV exposure was partially effective. Significant effects on intermediate objectives were observed. More research on the effectiveness of intervention in the field of WBV is needed.

Source: Adapted from C. Hulshof et al., *Occupational Environmental Medicine*, 2006, 63: 461–8.

Question: This was an outcomes evaluation, so it looked at 'Was WBV reduced?' If we now undertook a process evaluation, what might we look at?

2. **How a programme or intervention is working** – to feed into development of the programme, to ensure that it is working to best effect. This is usually called *process* or *formative* evaluation. It looks at how the intervention is formed or how the processes of the intervention come together, and focuses on the ways that a programme or intervention is working. This type of evaluation can be used to change different bits of the programme in order to improve it. Data collected will look at what happens

within the programme such as: the number of people invited compared with the number who actually attend; delays in the delivery of a service; the sex and age of the people who attend compared with the whole target group. It examines how the programme is implemented, and so might include data on how the programme is actually delivered when set against plans, for example, were planned exercise classes actually held? How many were cancelled? Why were cancelled classes not held and so on. Case Study 3.2 presents a summary of a process evaluation. This type of evaluation is often carried out by people working within the organisation that is running the intervention, who may be more likely to be in a position to be able to understand the processes and ask the best questions, as well to gather the data required to answer these questions. For example, routinely collected data supplemented with interviews or focus groups might be the best method to provide a real in-depth review. The service providers may be more honest with someone they are familiar with, and trust, than an external person. On the other hand, we also need to be aware that there may be personal issues between the evaluator and the evaluated. In every case, the participants need to be reassured that any information they give will be treated confidentially, and that data collection is separate from the management process. An information sheet and consent form should be used for people to sign up to the study (patients and staff) so that both commitment and responsibilities are understood by the data collectors and data providers.

CASE STUDY 3.2

Process evaluation: Improving respiratory infection control practices in family physicians' offices

Objective: To conduct a process evaluation of a short-term intervention for doctors to facilitate the introduction of new respiratory infection control practices in doctors' offices.

Methods: Five public health nurses went into 53 practices which contained 143 doctors. The nurses were facilitators in introducing new respiratory infection control practices in the local surgery. The effectiveness of the training given by the nurses was evaluated via questionnaires. Data assessing the process of facilitation were collected through activity logs and narrative reports. Physicians' satisfaction was assessed by questionnaire.

Findings: Nurse facilitators reported that training strongly contributed to their knowledge and skills, and all were satisfied with the training they delivered. All practices received at least two visits by the nurse facilitators, and 51 per cent had three or more visits. Nurse facilitors identified the provision of the evidence–based tool kit and consensus building with office staff as key factors in contributing to the interventions' success. Only 45 per cent (65/143) of doctors completed the questionnaire. Five percent reported they were somewhat dissatisfied with the intervention, 11 per cent reported the visits were not frequent enough, and 9 per cent stated that visits were too close together but 98 per cent would continue to use the service if it were available.

Conclusion: It is feasible for public health nurses to be trained in outreach facilitation to improve respiratory control practices in general practitioners' offices and this service is appreciated by the doctors.

Source: Adapted from P. Huston, W. Hogg, C. Martin, E. Soto, and A. Newbury, *Canadian Journal of Public Health*, 2006, 97 (6): 475–9.

Question: What did this evaluation do and why is this process evaluation?

3. **Whether the benefits of a programme are worth the costs**. The type of question this evaluation design answers is 'how much does it cost per unit of benefit?' For this type of evaluation we need to put a value on the benefits gained through the programme, as well as the costs of implementation and other impacts. For example, if a programme is successful, it might save resources in terms of reducing time off work, visits to health professionals, the costs of medication or hospital stays. However, there will have been costs associated with implementation – equipment purchased, materials used, staff involvement and possible additional training. Unanticipated costs may also result from the introduction of the new service, for example, a new demand for other services or additional patient (or health professional) travel costs. There are several different techniques that may be used to assess costs and benefits:

- A *cost minimisation analysis* will look at two ways of treating a patient, such as gas anaesthetic compared to injected anaesthetic (Case Study 1.2), and will only look at the cost of each (assuming they completely remove pain to the same extent).
- A *cost effectiveness analysis* will look at the cost of each unit of improvement in an outcome measure: for example, for each point reduction in a patient's pain level.
- A more complicated analysis is *cost utility analysis*, which looks at the cost of having additional years of life and the quality of life. The most common approach here is the notion of a quality adjusted life year for a person (QALY). A QALY is increasingly used in economic evaluations, given that it can be used across a variety of interventions and programmes and it enables comparisons to be made as to the relative value of a programme in one area when compared with an

intervention elsewhere (see Case Study 3.3). It combines the quality
of life and additional quantity of life in people who have a treatment
compared to those who do not have the same treatment.

- A less common approach is that of a *cost benefit analysis*. The problem with this method is that the benefits have to be translated into a
  monetary measure, and in the area of health this is extremely emotive
  and sensitive.

Cost effectiveness evaluation: The burden of ankylosing spondylitis and the cost-effectiveness of treatment with infliximab (Remicade)

Objectives: In the past, treatment options for ankylosing
spondylitis (AS) have been limited, and the introduction of new
treatments such as infliximab will have a noticeable impact on health
care budgets. The objective of this study therefore was to assess the
current burden of the disease and estimate the cost-effectiveness of
infliximab treatments.

Methods: Patients were sent a questionnaire to examine resource
consumption associated with disease severity. Mean costs were
estimated taking into account age, gender, disease duration, disease
activity and functional status, and disease development was
expressed as the annual progression of functional disability. The
cost-effectiveness of a new drug, infliximab, was estimated using the
results of a clinical trial in 70 patients.

Results: Fifty-seven per cent of patients answered the
questionnaires. The mean age was 57 (s.d. 11.2) years, 74 per cent
were male and mean disease duration was 30.2 (11.7) years. Mean
total costs were estimated at £6,765 (+/– £166) per year. Indirect
costs (for example, loss of earnings) represented 57.9 per cent, and
non-medical costs such as investments (for example, stair lifts,
modifications to car and home) and informal care (loss of work by
unpaid carer such as husband or wife) accounted for 16.5 per cent
of total costs. Mean costs for patients treated with standard care
were estimated at £25,128. For the infliximab-treated group, mean
costs (excluding treatment) were estimated at £17,240, a reduction
of 31 per cent. Thus, part of the infliximab cost was offset by
savings in other resources (£7,888), leaving an incremental cost of
£6,214. Treatment increased the number of quality-adjusted life
years (QALYs) by 0.175 QALYs, leading to a cost per QALY gained
of £35,400 for the first year of treatment. When treatment is
assumed to continue for the full two years, the cost per QALY is
£32,800. When infliximab infusions are given every eight weeks

instead of every six weeks, the cost per QALY is reduced to £17,300. In the long-term model, the cost per QALY is estimated at £9,600.

Conclusions: Non-medical costs and production losses dominate costs in AS, and economic evaluation must therefore adopt a societal perspective. The cost of treatment with infliximab is partly offset by reductions in the cost of the disease and patients' quality of life is increased, leading to a cost per QALY gained in the vicinity of £30,000 to £40,000 in the short term, but potentially below £10,000 in the long term.

Source: Taken from G. Kobelt et al., *Rheumatology*, 2004, 43 (9): 1158–66.

Question: What is a cost-effective evaluation measuring?

In undertaking economic evaluations it is advisable to get help from a health economist and to read a book specifically aimed at conducting economic evaluations (some references are given at the end of this chapter). The key to any evaluation looking at costs is that resources are scarce, so we need to work out a way of spending money that gives the most benefit. If we use resources for one treatment and this means they are not available for another treatment, this is called the opportunity cost. For instance, the opportunity cost of investing in a new exercise class may be that we cannot invest in reducing the waiting list for hip replacement surgery. In other words, funding is limited and a choice needs to be made between investing in one at the expense of the other. For this reason, we need to be clear about relative benefits and full costs. For example, we can use a set amount of money to prolong the life of 100 children with terminal cancer or the same amount of money to prevent one child being killed in a road traffic accident. Which use of the funding gives the most benefit?

In summary: The key to a useful and successful evaluation is to think about what the key question is in the particular case you are evaluating. Is it:

Does it work?
How does it work?
Are the benefits worth the costs?

Trying to answer many types of questions in one evaluation is not advisable in a small-scale study, as each requires the collection of a different kind of data. However, many studies do examine processes and outcomes within the same evaluation. Some evaluations may contain elements of all three types listed above, but we have to remember that the more evaluation objectives are set, and the more methods are planned to meet those objectives, the higher the cost of the evaluation will be.

Some more complex evaluations also explore a number of different levels and functions within organisations, but each sector of the evaluation needs to be clearly formulated to address the relevant questions. The evaluation can only be designed to examine areas where there is a focused question. Being clear about the key question means we can design our evaluation to ensure that we will have high-quality information concerning our central and most important question.

Evaluation methods

An evaluation can be designed to assess the delivery and effects of an intervention as it is implemented (observational design), or it can influence the way the intervention is set up so that, for instance, not everyone who could receive the new service is able to get it – but some have 'treatment as usual' until the effects of the new treatment are clear (this is called an experimental study).

There are some important choices to be made at the outset of the planning of an evaluation:

Is there an opportunity to work with the implementers of the new service/treatment to set up an experimental study?
If so, should I select people to receive the new treatment/service on a random basis or should this be done in a different way – for example, by area/practice/practitioner/time of day?
If not, is there a natural control group, for example, patients/service users, in another area that is similar in terms of case mix, where the service/treatment is not available, nor likely to be available during the period of evaluation?

The choices we make are directly related to the questions we wish to answer, and the resources we have available for the study. If we want to gather evidence that a treatment works, it is important to use an evaluation design that is fit for that purpose.

Is something effective?

It is important to consider how we will know whether a treatment is effective: if, say, 60 per cent of people show improvement following a treatment, would we say this is effective or not? It will depend on what would have happened otherwise. For this we need to identify a comparator, or control group. Randomised controlled trials are generally accepted as providing the best evidence concerning effectiveness. In this design, all those who could receive the treatment have an equal chance of being selected to receive the treatment, and any effects seen are therefore most likely to be due to the treatment rather than due to differences, for example, in age, illness severity or preferences, between groups. However, they are costly, difficult to set up and provide limited information concerning how a treatment worked – or didn't work. If it is not possible to allocate patients to a treatment group on a random basis, then another way of allocating patients may be considered. The outcomes of patients attending a neighbouring clinic where the treatment is not available could be useful. In this case it will be important to compare the characteristics of the patients in each group to see if they are similar or systematically different (one group, older, more ill?) before drawing conclusions about the effects of the new treatment based on a comparison of symptoms some time later.

Quantitative (assessment of numbers or quantities) and qualitative (assessment of text or quality) methods can be mixed together in a study design to answer questions about effects and processes, as long as the study resources are sufficient to cover the costs of carrying out the work.

In summary: To know if something is effective we need to have something to compare with the intervention. We need a control group or a group who did not receive the intervention.

Issues to consider when designing the evaluation

If we know what type of evaluation we are implementing, then we should have a better idea of what type of data we need to collect in order to answer our question. For example, an outcome or summative evaluation might have one specific question, such as 'has whole body vibration exposure been reduced?' (see Case Study 3.1). For this we need to collect some measure of whole body vibration exposure.

After determining the data we need to collect, we must think of the best way to collect the data items. The quality of the evaluation depends on the quality of the data that are collected. The data collected need to be:

- **Reliable**: This means the data can be trusted. If we measure the same thing twice, will we get the same answer? For example, if two different people measure the same patient's waist circumference, will they get the same answer? If one person measures the same waist circumference twice, will they get the same answer? What do we need to consider to ensure that we get the same answer on each occasion?
- **Valid**: This means it must measure what it says it measures. For example, if we weigh 100 people but do not calibrate the scales, the data might be reliable but are also reliably wrong, and therefore not valid. Another example of another type of validity would be about the best way to measure obesity: is it valid to collect data on body mass index (weight and height); should we collect measures of waist circumference or should we record body fat levels? What would be the most valid measure of obesity?

- **Representative and generalisable**: This means that the people we include in our evaluation actually reflect the people we want to represent. If we carry out an evaluation of an intervention for the fractured neck of femurs using a sample of people who have undergone hip replacement surgery, we cannot assume our findings will apply – or be generalisable – to people who have undergone other types of joint surgery. However, if our sample is both appropriately selected and large enough, findings can be used to inform the care of the whole population of those who have undergone hip replacement. Any limitations in how the sample was defined will, however, limit its generalisability; for example, if only people over the age of 75 are used in the evaluation, then the findings cannot be generalised to represent people aged 40 or 30; if the study was carried out in only one hospital, it is difficult to try and apply findings to patients treated elsewhere. The patients included in the study must be similar to those for whom findings are to be applied.

In the following section we describe ways in which we ensure that our data are reliable, valid and representative of the group we aim to include.

Making sure the data are reliable: repeatability

We need to make sure we have the correct reading of what we want to measure. A simple thing like waist circumference will be different depending on exactly where and how we measure; for example, if we measure it above or across or below the belly button, if we pull the measuring tape tight, or hold it loosely round the waist or allow the person themselves to do the measuring. If we measure the same person's waist circumference a number of times and the measurement changes or varies, is this because the person lost or gained weight or because our measurements are not very reliable? One way to improve reliability is to write a protocol of how we want something measured, and to pilot the protocol across data collectors.

Reliability can be threatened by low *intra-rater reliability* or low *inter-rater reliability. Both need to be high, if our data are to be reliable.* Intra-rater reliability refers to the degree of difference between measures taken by one person of the same thing on several different occasions (for example, we ask someone to measure the same waist circumference on several different days). Inter-rater reliability refers to the degree of difference between measures of the same thing taken by different people (for example, we get several different people independently to measure the same waist circumference and see how much the measurements differ). We should calculate and report the inter-rater and the intra-rater reliability in our evaluation. This gives the readers an estimate of the reliability of the data.

Making sure the data are valid: bias

We need to make sure that the data we collect are a true reflection of what we want to measure. There are many reasons why the data collected may not be valid.

One example would be that the data collected does not measure what it reports to measure. For example, as a measure of fitness, we ask a group of teenagers to run on a tread mill for five minutes. If they give up before five minutes (perhaps because they are bored), we will record that they are unfit. However, they could actually be very fit and had we asked them to do turns and jumps with a skate board, they may well have carried on for an hour. The measure that was selected to assess fitness was inappropriate (for the sample of teenagers), and does not measure what it says it measures – namely, it is not a valid measure, on its own, of fitness.

Another example of a measure with low validity in some populations could be a postal questionnaire that automatically excludes everyone who cannot read and write well (perhaps because of language, literacy or physical limitations, such as a hand injury or an eye problem). We can exclude all those who cannot read and write English, as well as all those people who just have not got the time or the interest to complete a questionnaire. People who do not respond to the questionnaire may be very different from those who do respond. Missing their experiences, opinions and views will mean the findings are based on the self-selected group of people who complete and return their questionnaires. This is called non-response bias, and will have the most serious impact on validity and reliability in the case of a low response rate, or where those who respond have very different views from those who do not. In this case, one way to try to address the problem is to compare the characteristics that we already hold from a different source (for example, age, sex, condition) of the people who responded with those who did not respond. If the responders and non-responders do not appear to differ across a range of characteristics, then we may feel more confident that in these respects our respondents were representative of the whole group. This may give us confidence in the validity of our findings for the whole group – although it does not rule out the possibility that views expressed through the questionnaire itself might be different between those who replied and those who did not, and these cannot be checked across the groups. Therefore, when doing an evaluation we should report on the non-responders as well as the responders. We should justify why our methods are valid indicators of what they report to measure and support this by references to other people's evaluations (from our background reading).

This brings us on to how we sample or select a representative group of people.

Making sure the data are representative and generalisable: sampling

It is neither feasible nor necessary to include everybody in our evaluation. It is not a good use of resources to include more people than we need to in any evaluation. We therefore use the strategy of sampling – selecting a group of people to represent the whole group that we are interested in. We aim to use the information we get about people in this sample to inform our understanding of the whole group, and how a service or treatment affects people in the whole group. This can be through generalising findings to everyone, or, in qualitative research, by collecting data until the whole range of responses can reasonably be assumed to have been gathered. But, in order to generalise, the sample needs to be representative of everyone. For example, we cannot send a questionnaire to ten retired, female health visitors and say that their responses represent all the people providing care in the community, male and female, retired and working, or even all female, retired health visitors. This is because this is a very small and select sample.

To make sure our sample is representative we need to:

- define who our sample should be representing: who is it within the population that we wish the study findings to be applicable to?
- write a list of the characteristics of our sample, including where we might recruit participants - this is called a sampling frame.
- define a method which will select individuals so that our sample will reflect the population.

For example, if we want to be able to describe the opinions of people involved in delivering care in the community (see Case Study 3.4), our population (the people we should be sampling from) are not general health professionals, or patients or relatives of patients, but will be more specific and will include social workers, home carers, health visitors, midwives, district nurses and ambulance crews.

CASE STUDY 3.4

Evaluation of training needs within the community

Aims: To provide a description of the training needs of agencies who provide care in the community.

Methods: A self-completion questionnaire was sent to 65 individuals involved in delivering community care. Individuals were selected from health visitors, home helps, midwives, private care companies, social workers, ambulance crews and councillors.

Findings: We achieved an 80 per cent response rate (52/65). Key findings included (1) a lack of adequate training for both management and direct care staff, (2) a need for multidisciplinary training, (3) a lack of mentoring or the passing on of skills from experienced staff to new staff, (4) a lack of time or finance for adequate training, (5) a perceived lack of recognition of the importance of training by management staff.

Conclusion: The responses received suggested a general lack of ability to undertake training due to time and financial constraints and a lack of understanding of the need for training by management staff.

Question: What would you say could be the bias in this evaluation?

What type of place should we go to get their views? We might go to: GP surgeries, social services, home help agencies, the ambulance service (our sampling frame).

It is probably not feasible to include all those people delivering community care, so we need a way of identifying some representative individuals and then asking them what they think. Some methods are:

Random sampling: This is a method by which every eligible person has an equal chance of being selected for the sample, in the same way that every lottery ticket owner has an equal chance of winning. It can be done by writing everyone's name on a bit of paper, putting all the papers in a box and then picking out (without looking) which ones will 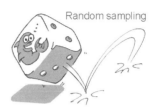 be included in the sample. However, the standard way to identify a random sample is to:

- Give everyone a number. For this we need to identify everyone in the population and give them each a number. This is the *Person's ID Number*.
- Make a set of random numbers. A calculator or computer can generate a set of random numbers, or you can get random numbers from www. randomization.com. This is just a set of random numbers generated by a computer. This is the *Random Number List*. (If you want to know more about different way of randomising, go to www.sealedenvelope.com/tse/ protocols.php).
- The list of random numbers tells you which individuals are included in the sample. If the random number list is 2, 18, 36, 42 and 46, then the people with the ID numbers 2, 18, 36, 42 and 46 will be invited to take part in the evaluation. These are the people in the sample.

Quota sampling or purposive sampling: This ensures that certain types of people are included in the sample (with a random sample there is always a chance that some groups may be excluded, particularly if the sample – or the group we are interested in – is small). We might do this if we want to reproduce the proportions of groups within the population. For example, if the population we are interested in is composed of equal numbers of men and women, we might want ten men and ten women, and if half of the women in the population we have identified are midwives and half are social workers, we might select five midwives and five social service workers; we might then decide that age is a factor we need to consider and thus select ten aged 20–39, and ten others aged 40–65. Within this approach, individuals may still be selected randomly using the method described above within each group, for example, once for men and again for women; once for midwives and again for social workers.

Convenience sampling: This is sometimes used in situations where it is difficult to recruit patients or other participants and time is short. For example, patients who attend a particular clinic on a particular occasion and consent to participate can be recruited in to the study in order to get an idea quickly of the range of issues and experiences that the group of patients has encountered. However, generalising from the findings of this type of sample is problematic.

Systematic sampling: This consists of selecting systematically every tenth or fiftieth (or any defined number) person who is eligible for the study. The method may be used in a clinic situation where we want to select patients and so we can take perhaps every tenth person attending out-patients, although it is always important to check whether any bias, for example, time of day, is being introduced through the sampling method used.

In summary: There are a number of types of sampling which need to be considered in order to select the method that is practical and best meets the evaluation aims. In random sampling, each member of the population identified has an equal chance of being chosen. In purposive, quota or convenience sampling, the researcher selects who is in the sample and each member of the relevant population does not have an equal chance of being included. Sampling methods can be combined in any study, but it is very important to be absolutely clear about how any sample has been identified, and to be able to describe the method clearly in the evaluation report.

Summary

- The design of the evaluation is determined by the questions it aims to answer, the resources available and the audience to whom it is addressed.
- The design of the evaluation determines what data items are collected.
- A summative or outcome evaluation collects data on the effects the programme or intervention has had.
- A formative or process evaluation collects data on how a programme or intervention is working.
- A cost-effectiveness evaluation balances those data concerning the impact of an intervention with other data concerning how much it has cost, and about any cost savings or impacts in other areas that have resulted from its introduction.
- An evaluation can be internal, external, or participatory.
- The evaluation should be designed and planned to make sure that the data collected are repeatable, valid and representative.

Frequently asked questions

How do I know if I have the best design for the evaluation I want to do?

An important part of the design and planning process is consultation with patients/service users and stakeholders. This consultation process can reveal the potential problems of feasibility or validity. When we know the design and what we want to do, then we can do a small test run (which is called a 'pilot') of the evaluation to see if there are any problems and if we get the data we expect and want.

I want to carry out a small-scale evaluation but need to provide some evidence about the impact of the service I am evaluating – what approach should I take?

First, it is important to be clear about the evidence base for the service by identifying, reading and appraising previous research studies on the topic. The second step is to define what is meant by impact – in terms of what, and for whom? The size of the impact that it is important to detect should be decided, and a sample size calculation carried out so that you know how many people you will need to include in order to have a reasonable chance of detecting this difference. You then need to consider the feasibility of carrying out a study of this size – in terms of the throughput of patients (how long will the study period need to be?), and the resources needed to carry out data collection and analysis. Finally, consider all the options – would a process evaluation be more achievable? Or a qualitative approach?

I think we can just about afford to run a randomised controlled trial to test the effectiveness of this new intervention, but I will have to carry out the analysis myself – what advice would you give me?

Seek advice from a statistician at an early stage, and be careful not to underestimate the resources required to run a trial. It may be better to use a simpler study design that you will be able to carry out well, rather than stretching yourself and your team and runnning the risk of not delivering the evaluation due to unforeseen problems.

We have been asked to evaluate our programme but we know that some aspects are not working as they should, although we don't know why. How should we address this in our evaluation?

This may give you an opportunity to gather data about how things are working and to look at patterns in the data. For example, if there is a concern about waiting times, gather data about waiting times in general and calculate the mean, median, and range overall, as well for different times of the day/days of the week/clinics and so on. This may help you to understand a little more about where the problems lie. Qualitative interviews could follow the analysis of routine data, with, for example, clinicians or patients, in order to understand in more detail why these delays arise, and their effects. Even in an evaluation like this, it is important to clearly describe your plan, or protocol, with aims, objectives, methods and a plan of analysis.

In addition, the views of experts or external peers can be sought – through informal contacts or through the local NHS R&D offices. One reason for developing an explicit plan or protocol for the evaluation (see Chapter 4) is to ensure that all the foreseeable obstacles can be identified and appropriately addressed at the beginning of the evaluation.

Further reading

Philip Clarke, Alastair Gray, Jane Wolstenholme and Sarah Worsworth (forthcoming) *Applied Methods of Cost-effectiveness Analysis in Health Care.* Oxford: HERC.

M. Drummond, M. Sculpher, G. Torrance, B. O'Brien and G. Stoddart (2005) *Methods for Economic Evaluation of Health Care Programmes*, 3rd edn. Oxford: Oxford University Press.

D. Kernick (2005) An introduction to the basic principles of health economics for those involved in the development and delivery of headache care, *Cephalalgia*, 25 (9): 709–14.

C.J. Phillips (2005) *Health Economics: An introduction for health professionals.* Oxford: Blackwell/BMJ Books.

A. Shiell, C. Donaldson, C. Mitton and G. Currie (2002) Health economic evaluation, *Journal of Epidemiology and Community Health*, 56: 85–8.

Web pages
www.evidence-based-medicine.co.uk/ebmfiles/WhatisaQALY.pdf
www.evidence-based-medicine.co.uk/ebmfiles/Whatiscosteffect.pdf
http://ag.arizona.edu/fcs/cyfernet/cyfar/Costben2.htm
www.nsf.gov/ehr/rec/evaldesign.jsp
http://bmj.bmjjournals.com/epidem/epid.html
www.socialresearchmethods.net/kb/desexper.php

4 How to Plan an Evaluation

Why plan?

It is tempting when starting an evaluation to jump straight in and begin data collection without a clear written plan – or protocol – for the evaluation. It can seem easier to collect everything that we can about a service and its delivery, with perhaps one or two added things like a questionnaire or form for clinicians, than to sit down at the outset and define each data item, where we can get it and what it will be used for. However, taking this approach, without taking time to sit down and plan each stage thoroughly, can lead us to much more work in the end. The initial stages of planning an evaluation can be quite a frustrating time, because we are usually really keen to get on with the project and to dive into the 'meaty' part of it – collecting and analysing the data to find out the results as quickly as possible. This, perhaps, could be likened to going shopping without a list – and when feeling hungry, we are likely to come back with a trolley full of goodies that we fancied as we went around the supermarket, but lacking the essentials that we need because we forgot about them! It is easy to make the mistake of collecting all the data we can, hoping that in the end we will have enough to complete the evaluation. However, this means we may collect things we will not need, may never use and will not are sure how to analyse. On the other hand, without clear planning of the detail of the evaluation and the data collection, we may only realise later on in the process that we need some data items that are not available, or that we have not gathered, or that we have collected but in the wrong format.

Conducting the evaluation like this can waste a great deal of time and money, is likely to result in no clear answers, and runs the risk of annoying all those people who have given their time to the evaluation. This will threaten future work: the people we need to participate or support us to carry out evaluations are usually busy people, who may not find the time to get involved a second time around if their first experience is not good. Therefore, we should plan in order to make sure we have a clear idea of what we are doing, what data we need to collect, and how we are going to analyse these.

In this chapter we will outline why it is important to clearly plan our evaluation, and how to go about the planning process. We will then discuss what should go into an evaluation plan, including the detail about each section of the protocol; and finally, how to use it to successfully complete our evaluation.

What does a plan do?

It is vitally important to draft an evaluation plan, to agree this with all those involved or affected, and to stick to the plan as far as possible, making note of any changes (and the reasons for them) to the agreed protocol as the evaluation gets underway. This helps enormously with ensuring that:

- the aims and objectives of the evaluation are clearly and appropriately defined
- we can *access the data* we need to meet our evaluation objectives
- we collect the *right data* to address our evaluation objectives
- the data are in the *right form* to enable us to carry out the appropriate analysis to answer our evaluation questions
- we collect *enough data* to answer our evaluation questions
- the *right people* are engaged to ensure the evaluation is a success
- we have *enough time and resources* to carry out the evaluation
- we create opportunities to participate in the planning of the implementation of initiatives alongside the evaluation, and that these are maximised to ensure that the best evaluation design is adopted.

In general, evaluation needs to be part of the process of delivering the service. If it is planned from the beginning, it will take much less time and money to complete the evaluation. Planning involves really thinking about what the evaluation objectives are, and how these will be achieved. With a plan we have a clear idea of what we want to do and how we will achieve it.

How do we go about planning?

It is really important to do the planning as a team exercise – it is not something we can dream up while sitting alone at our desks. We will always need input from those with different areas of expertise; in a health care evaluation this will vary between projects, but is likely to include:

- Clinicians – doctors, nurses, other professionals delivering care (paramedics/occupational therapists/physiotherapists etc)
- Managers
- Frontline staff

- Service users
- People with other specialist skills – for example, information technology, statistics
- Clerical support.

It can be challenging to identify and recruit appropriate people to include in the group. Although we may agree that it would be useful to include a front-line staff member on the team, how do we go about getting that person in a way that is equitable for staff and effective for the team? With the support of senior management, it may be possible to advertise the opportunity amongst those eligible, with details of both the role and the qualities sought, and to invite applications which can then be anonymously assessed. This has been done successfully within the ambulance service, where represen-tation from paramedics and technicians has been sought for local audit projects (see Figure 4.1). Applications were invited from frontline staff interested in participating as team members for the audit, open to all cur-rent frontline staff in the service. The role and commitment were described, and the personal qualifications and qualities detailed. Those interested were invited to submit a one-page outline of how they felt they could con-tribute to the audit through membership of the team. The successful appli-cants were then supported by their local line managers to attend meetings.

Are you interested in helping to improve the quality of prehospital care for asthma patients?

We are looking for one paramedic and one technician to join the Steering Group for a clinical audit of the care of patients with acute asthma, to represent the perspective, views and expe-rience of frontline staff.
   Other members of the Steering Group will include:

- a Medical Director of xx Ambulance Service
- a Respiratory Physician
- a GP
- a Specialist asthma nurse
- an A&E consultant
- a Patient representative
- an Ambulance Service trainer
- a Clinical Audit co-ordinator

We are looking for frontline staff with experience of attending patients with acute asthma, who have an interest in improving care for patients with this condition. Some understanding of research and clinical audit methods would be desirable.
   Meetings will be held quarterly over the one-year period of the audit. All travel expenses will be paid, and your manager will allow you to attend during work time or, where necessary, through overtime payment.
   If you would like to join this group, please send a brief outline of why you are interested, and how you believe you could contribute to the project, to xx, by xx/xx/xx.

Figure 4.1   Advertisement to recruit steering group participants

It is important to agree roles and responsibilities for the planning and undertaking of the evaluation:

- Who will be drafting the plan?
- Who will be carrying out the data collection?

- Who will be undertaking analysis of the data?
- Who has responsibility for the delivery of the final report from the evaluation?
- What is the role of the group – is it advisory or steering?
- How will the group members be involved?
- What is the anticipated time commitment?
- What will the members get from being involved?

It is important to discuss and agree these points at the first meeting of the evaluation team, as well as to start planning the evaluation itself. It may be helpful to present an outline proposal to the group and allow the opportunity for comment and discussion about each aspect of the plan, before further work is undertaken to develop the outline to what we call a full protocol, which will then guide the evaluation. The team must also be offered the opportunity to identify others who should be invited to participate. An inclusive approach is often more likely to lead to a strong product. Although it can sometimes be uncomfortable to raise issues about which people do not agree, it is much better to go through these questions at an early stage. We can take the advice of people with different perspectives, and provide a forum in which people who have different views can express these views and come to some consensus about how the evaluation should proceed. This will often work better than keeping the evaluation 'under wraps' until data collection is underway or even until findings are published. If a wide range of participants is included throughout the evaluation, the report is much less likely to contain inaccuracies or to have overlooked the point of view of key stakeholders. In addition, if the evaluation is a success, this model of good practice can be spread further throughout the organisation, and the people involved are likely to act as natural 'champions' or salespeople for the evaluation, making it easier to then implement change as a result of evaluation findings. Although it may seem costly in terms of people's time, this inclusive approach can be very helpful and may sometimes save resources in the longer term as the evaluation will be 'embedded' in the running of the service and people are more likely to feel ownership of the project and its results.

In summary: When drawing up our plan we should get input and advice from a team of people and we should agree roles and responsibilities from the beginning.

Walking through our plan

As we make the plan it is important to visualise how we will actually perform each part of the evaluation. Imagine completing each bit, how we might approach patients, how the questionnaires will be collected and who will be responsible for collecting and recording returned questionnaires. If we mentally walk through each aspect of the evaluation as if we are doing it now, we can often identify where problems might lie in advance and overcome them before they occur. As we actually think about doing each aspect of the evaluation as if we were about to do it now, we can jot down what problems there might be. For example, if we want to look at patients' notes, we might feel that in clinic is an ideal time to read through them (as the notes are already available). However, will there be the time between patients to do it at this point, or would it be better to spend one complete day pulling all the notes for every patient in the study and reading through them in bulk?

When we come to write a plan and actually put it in on paper as a document, this document is called a *protocol*.

What should go into our evaluation protocol?

The protocol for our evaluation will need to contain some basic elements, but can be modified for local use as befits the topic of the evaluation. We would expect, however, for there to be certain common elements, even if these are sometimes called different things:

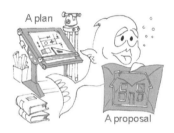

- Title
- Evaluation team
- Acknowledgement of funding
- Background
- Evaluation aims and objectives
- Evaluation design/methods

  - Overall approach
  - Measures to be used
  - Data items and sources
  - Sample size(s)
  - Analysis plan

- Timescales
- Resources
- Project management
- Outputs
- References

We will discuss in some detail now what we would normally include in each of these sections.

Title

This should be a short sentence that explains what we will be doing. For example, 'Developing a rapid access chest pain clinic: patients' needs and experiences' (see Case Study 4.1).

A nurse-led rapid access chest pain clinic – experience from the first three years

Background: The clinical presentation of chest pain is a major problem for primary health care professionals. Rapid access chest pain clinics (RACPC) enable quick assessment, investigation and formation of a treatment plan for such patients without a waiting list. We have been running a nurse-led RACPC for three years and are evaluating the performance of this clinic.

Process: Patients are seen within two weeks of referral. An electrocardiogram (ECG) is recorded on arrival in the clinic and the patient is examined to see if further investigation is required.

Analysis of results: Four hundred and fifty-four patients were seen in the clinic from January 2001–December 2003. Three hundred and twenty-four patients (71.4 per cent) underwent exercise testing, of which 54 (16.7 per cent) had a positive result. One hundred and thirteen patients (24.9 per cent) were referred for angiography. Of these, 75 (66.4 per cent) had coronary heart disease. Thirty-three patients (29.2 per cent) have undergone percutaneous coronary intervention (PCI) and 19 (16.8 per cent) have required coronary artery bypass grafting (CABG). Twenty-three patients (20.4 per cent) are being treated medically. Satisfaction with the service offered by the clinic was high, evidenced by the results of questionnaires sent to patients.

Conclusion: This paper demonstrates that these clinics offer patients rapid access to assessment of their chest pain and they are well accepted by the patients attending the clinic.

Source: adapted from A. Pottle et al., *European Journal of Cardiovascular Nursing*, 2005, 4 (3): 227–33.

Question: Is this a process evaluation or an outcomes evaluation?

Evaluation team

As described above, we would expect our evaluation team to include a variety of people who are involved in, or likely to be affected by, the evaluation or its findings. With their agreement, it is useful to name these participants. This then acts as a written record of the commitment of those individuals, which is useful for keeping people engaged as well as to show others who is involved in order to gain support for the study.

It is good practice to name all members of the evaluation team as authors on the final report from the evaluation. We would discuss and agree this expectation at the outset, and then ensure that all named members of the team are kept in touch with progress throughout the evaluation, and have the opportunity to contribute at all stages, in particular when findings are interpreted and written up.

Acknowledgement of funding

We would usually include a brief statement indicating whether the funding for the evaluation came from internal sources or whether there was any external support. Any conflict of interests should be declared, for example, any financial interests that any team members have in the intervention being evaluated. This allows anyone who reads the final evaluation report to understand any potential sources of bias, and how they have been dealt with. Any such interests that emerge later on could be extremely damaging to the evaluation and reduce its chances of being influential, even if they had been dealt with appropriately during the study. For further information refer to the BMJ website, where competing interest rules are clearly described: http://resources.bmj.com/bmj/authors/checklists-forms/competing-interests.

Background

It is helpful to set out the context for the study, and the reasons for carrying out the evaluation. Although these may seem quite clear to those closely involved, it is a good idea to describe this background clearly, so that the document can be used to draw in key participants from outside the core group, for example, from a related service, or a service user representative. An explanation of the context for the study – in terms of policy and practice – may be very helpful for those who are not directly involved in service provision in the area. In addition, there may be many reasons for focussing on a particular area for evaluation, some of which may be more apparent than others. Various people who are involved may have different ideas or understandings of why the evaluation is being set up. Without a shared and explicit understanding, it will be difficult to agree on the evaluation's objectives, methods and measures of success. Having the context and rationale written down in black and white will help to identify points about which people have different understandings, and to iron these out before progressing with the rest of the plan.

It is in this section, also, that the research evidence concerning best care for the condition or about the effectiveness of the intervention should be summarised. It is here that we write briefly about what is already known about how well the treatment or service that we plan to evaluate works – or about what is known about the patient group at whom the intervention is aimed. The basis on which the intervention is being introduced should be made clear – this will help with clarifying the aim and objectives of the evaluation. For instance, there might be clear evidence that an intervention is effective, for example, aspirin for myocardial infarction. Our evaluation might be to examine the introduction of aspirin by paramedics in emergency ambulances. If this is our evaluation, then we do not need to focus on patient health outcomes (death, damage to the heart, etc), but should look at:

- whether the right patients are given the drug
- the time interval between their 999 call and when they receive the aspirin
- other aspects of interest about how the new treatment is delivered.

In summary: Background information should put the aims of our evaluation in context. In addition, the background should state the reason for doing the evaluation, in the context of current health policy. For example (see also Case Study 4.1):

Rapid access chest pain clinics have swiftly been established throughout England since their recommendation in the National Service Framework for Coronary Heart Disease [1]. However, there remains considerable uncertainty about the effectiveness, cost-effectiveness and optimal procedures of these clinics [2]. The Department of Health promotes user involvement in health service development [3] and the Fifth Report on Provision of Services for Patients with Heart Disease [4] has identified the patient's perspective as an important factor in the design and delivery of effective cardiac services.

References:
1. Department of Health (2000) *National Service Framework for Coronary Heart Disease: Modern Standards and Service Models.* London: Department of Health.
2. Chest pain clinics: hope or hype? *International Journal of Clinical Practice,* 2002, 56: 4–5.
3. Department of Health (2004) *Patient and Public Involvement in Health: The evidence for policy implementation.* London: Department of Health.
4. British Cardiac Society and Royal College of Physicians. Fifth report on the provision of services for patients with heart disease. *Heart,* 2002, 88 (Suppl 3): 1–56.

When writing the background it is important to stay focussed on the evaluation that is proposed. Some detail about the context is needed to help those less familiar with the topic to understand, for example, the relevant features of national policy, local service delivery arrangements or about the population where the evaluation is due to take place. It is easy, however, to put too much detail in this section, and to stray too far from the point. The decision about what to include and what is too much information will need to be based on some thought about who the document is for and what they will need to know.

We need to remember the purpose of the background section – to describe the context for the evaluation and to explain why the evaluation is being set up – and check this each time we start writing a new paragraph.

Evaluation aim and objectives

This is perhaps the most important section of the evaluation plan – the overall aim and objectives of the study. These can be written as primary and secondary (or subsidiary) evaluation questions. This section is key to everything that follows. However, it is also a section that is easy to overlook or undervalue. The importance of 'nailing' the aim and objectives cannot be overstressed. Each word will count and should be considered carefully before agreement. Every other section of the protocol will be built around the aim and objectives of the evaluation – the background sets the scene and should justify the questions. The methods need to be set up to meet *in full* the aim and objectives, and to *not go outside* them. There needs to be a perfect match between the aim, objectives and methods to ensure that the data collected can answer the evaluation questions.

Throughout the evaluation, the aim and objectives guide our work. It is easy to get a little lost during the data collection or analysis phases of the study – we start to not be able to 'see the wood for the trees' and often discover new avenues we hadn't foreseen. The aim and objectives, if described appropriately and matched properly to our methods, will help us to find our way again. There are always numerous interesting questions that surround any topic, and research holds out the tempting opportunity to explore any number of these as we collect data around the topic. Although such opportunities can be exploited, it is important to not lose sight of our original purpose – otherwise our final evaluation report may end up as a jumble of interesting analyses, but will not meet our agreed evaluation aim and objectives.

Defining our evaluation aim and objectives takes more than one attempt. Although we may feel we know what we want to do, and why, often when we try to state explicitly the questions we want to answer, we realise that we are not quite as clear as we had thought, and also that others who are key to the process may not have exactly the same ideas in mind. It is important not to let any differences in viewpoint result in vague aims that are actually impossible to answer – this would be a recipe for an evaluation that, at the end of the day, does not fully meet anyone's needs, and also will result in some disappointment to those participants whose expectations have not been met.

The overall aim should therefore be a short, clear statement of what the evaluation will try to do.

Within the overall aim, it is often useful to describe objectives. These are rather narrower statements of what the evaluation will try to achieve in order to meet the overall aim. For example:

Aim: To evaluate the rapid access chest pain clinic from the point of view of patients

Objectives:
1. To examine the patients' experiences of attending the rapid access chest pain clinic
2. To identify areas where the clinic could be improved according to patients
3. To explore how the patients would recommend making these improvements to the clinic

The objectives should add up to the aim – not to less or more than the aim.

Evaluation design/methods

In this section of the protocol it is important to describe the overall approach to the evaluation, and then to further describe in detail the ways that the evaluation aim and objectives will be met.

Overall approach: It is helpful to begin this section with a summary of what is intended, for example, 'The evaluation will adopt a mixed methods approach, using a combination of routine data sources and semi-structured interviews to gather the data'.

Measures to be used: The measures that will be used to answer the evaluation questions need to be stated. We can divide what we are measuring into categories of structure (the set up of the situation), process (how things are done) and outcome (what the result was). For example, in the case of an evaluation of pre-hospital aspirin administration (see Case Study 4.2):

Structure: Were all patients attended by a paramedic-staffed ambulance?
Process: What proportion of patients who met the criteria for administration of aspirin received the drug?
            What was the time interval between the 999 call and administration of aspirin?
Outcome: Were patients happy to receive aspirin from their attending ambulance crew?

CASE STUDY 4.2

Emergency pre-hospital treatment of suspected acute myocardial infarction – adjusting the focus

Background: The evidence surrounding the emergency pre-hospital care of patients with acute myocardial infarction (AMI) is well established. Early administration of aspirin and thrombolytic treatment for appropriate patients saves lives. National standards are now being proposed which state that suspected heart attack victims should receive aspirin if indicated, and that thrombolysis should be given within 60 minutes of calling for professional help.

Objectives: To measure current ambulance service performance against the proposed standards of care.

Methods: Retrospective criteria-based audit of 100 randomly sampled patient report forms completed by ambulance crews coded as 'chest pain' from December 1998.

Results: Approximately 20 per cent (n = 19) of patients were attended within eight minutes. All frontline vehicles are defibrillator equipped and all frontline staff are trained to use them. The attending crew administered aspirin to 72 patients. Ten had already taken aspirin and contraindications were recorded for a further five. In 13 cases no aspirin was documented as having been given, with no reason for non-treatment recorded. An average of 46 minutes elapsed between the call to the ambulance service and the arrival of a patient at the accident and emergency department.

Discussion: The availability of evidence does not necessarily ensure optimal patient care. Although the study showed a high rate of appropriate aspirin administration, there is a clear area for improvement. The national standards will serve to focus emergency care onto the additional priorities of timeliness of treatment and interface with general practitioners.

Source: 'Emergency pre-hospital treatment of suspected acute myocardial infarction – adjusting the focus' (abstract), P. Clarke, H. Snooks and Y. Palmer, *Pre-hospital Immediate Care*, 1999; 3: 177.

Question: What is this? Is it a process evaluation, outcomes evaluation, service evaluation or audit? Does it need ethical approval?

Data items and sources: It is important to think about where all the data that are needed for the evaluation will come from. Some of the data may be already available, for example, from medical records or computerised admission details. Some may need to be added, such as an additional form for nurses, or an additional question that receptionists need to ask and record on the admission details. Some data may need to be collected directly from patients or service users and might involve questionnaires or interviews.

In the aspirin example above, the information about staffing may come from centralised routine records; the data concerning aspirin administration will come from routine clinical information completed by crews when they attend patients; the information about patient satisfaction will need to be collected for the evaluation through a questionnaire or by a researcher talking to patients.

In each case, we need to think through the processes by which the data are accessed and gathered for the evaluation. Centralised routine data (medical notes, laboratory tests etc) can probably most easily be captured – but we can't make any assumptions about their availability or quality! We need to find out where each data item is stored, and how, and agree by what manner we will access the information in order to meet the needs of the evaluation, with the relevant personnel.

In summary: We not only need to plan what data we want to collect, we need to plan where and how we will get these data. We need to look at the quality of existing data (medical notes and records) and see if we need to supplement this with extra data collection (new forms, questionnaires or tests).

Sample size(s):   The sample size we aim to reach needs to be planned alongside the definition of aims and objectives and methods. We need to be realistic about what we can achieve – with study resources and taking into account constraints such as numbers of patients with the targeted condition who attend per week (throughput of patients). It is easy to be overambitious about the numbers we can include. We need to think about the implications of recruitment for each subsequent part of the study – can we keep up with the retrieval of medical records and patient follow-up planned? We have to remember that if we are sending out questionnaires, we will need to keep track of those who respond and those who do not, and send out reminders, then input completed questionnaires onto our database, and check the quality of inputted data before carrying out an analysis. We also need to be realistic about how many patients or service users we can include from the point of view of the volume of cases – once again, it is easy to be overambitious about this. It is best to check how many of those patients with the targeted condition, and of the specified age range, come into contact with the service, for instance, each month. We need to remember that some patients will be lost to the study – some people will be missed by clinic staff or through information systems, some will not consent to participate, some records will be missing and some patients will not respond despite having agreed to participate. All these factors should be taken into account when calculating a realistic sample size for the study. The size that can be achieved will guide your definition of your research questions – it is pointless setting your research questions as ones which cannot be answered by the sample that you can recruit. Many studies, unfortunately, suffer from being *underpowered* – with the numbers included, even if a difference of clinical or operational importance did exist between study groups, there is a good chance it would be missed. A study like this is wasting everyone's time and energy and can be quite misleading. We can avoid this by calculating our sample size in advance – we usually consult with a statistician to do this (or use an online calculator, if we know what we are doing; see, for example, the website and Chapter 7). A sample size statement might look like the one below (this was taken from an evaluation of the introduction of new protocols for salbutamol administration by emergency ambulance personnel, Case Study 4.2):

'In order to have a 90 per cent chance of detecting an increase of 25 per cent in salbutamol administration from the current 58 per cent, the sample size required for the evaluation at the 5 per cent level of significance is 227.'

Generally speaking, the smaller the difference we are looking for, the larger the sample size needs to be. If we are unable realistically to recruit the numbers required to answer the question of interest within the timescale and resources available for the evaluation, we must revise our question and ensure that all the participants understand and agree to the new question.

In a qualitative study (one collecting data through interviews or focus groups), sample size is important but will be governed by different considerations. It is quite possible to recruit a small sample in order to explore the range of views or experiences of these patients. However, although numbers may be smaller, the depth of data collected can make this type of data collection and analysis very time consuming.

In general, sampling techniques and numbers to be included need to be planned from the outset, and must match with the aim and objectives of the study to ensure that the questions set for the evaluation can be answered by the proposed methods.

Analysis plan: Again, it is tempting to stop planning at the data collection stage. We may think we can put off thinking about what we will do with our data until we have got these, as if somehow everything becomes clear at that point. It may just happen– but we may not then have the data we need to carry out the required analysis. It is at the planning stage that we need to think about our plans for analysis and describe these explicitly so that the link between aims/objectives, methods and analysis is clear.

Our analysis plan will be guided by the aims and objectives we have set for the evaluation. All the analyses planned should contribute to meeting these. If we find that we would like to do some further analyses, we should reconsider our objectives and perhaps amend them to accommodate the proposed analyses. If, however, they fall outside the overall aim of the study, it is probably best to plan to carry out these additional analyses in another project.

The analysis plan should cover all the data items – both qualitative (interviews/focus groups) and quantitative (numbers and quantities). If we are unsure about what we will do with our data, we should ask for advice at the beginning of the study, not once the data are collected and inputted or stored – it will be too late then to make any changes to the way in which the data are gathered.

An analysis plan is simply a record of what analysis we will undertake with our data. For example, we will compare the proportion of patients receiving aspirin in our area with the national average using a chi-squared test. An analysis plan is a statement of what we are going to do when we get all our data together.

Timescales

There should be a clear project plan, including projected timescales. It is only through explicitly describing how, when and who will carry out various tasks associated with the research, that we can really be sure that the project is achievable.

Time should be built in for consultation and gaining necessary permissions; for preparing and piloting; for gathering all the data including the follow up; for analysis; and for writing up the evaluation. Typically, we will probably not leave enough time for the latter stages – and by the time there is some slippage at the beginning, we will often find ourselves squashing the analysis, interpretation and write-up into a very tight timescale. It is difficult to then consult fully, by circulating drafts of the write-up of findings and conclusions, as the timescales are so short – or we will end up finishing late.

How long will it take?

The timetable can be plotted as seen in Figure 4.2 (this is called a Gantt chart) or may just consist of a series of statements, for example:

The study will be conducted within two years:

Months 0–3: Design advertising material and interview schedule.
Months 4–6: Recruit patients and conduct interviews.
Etc.

What do we want to show or evaluate?

1. To examine the patients' experience of the clinic.
2. To examine how patients would improve the clinic.

What difference will it make?

Give recommendations for improvement of the clinic according to the patients' experience.

What data need to be collected to reflect what you want to show?

Patients will be interviewed to find out their experiences of the clinic.
Patients will be telephoned to give their experiences using a telephone interview.

Are sources of data reliable and valid for the aim we are trying to show?

Patients will be asked to participate as they arrive in the early stages of the study. Then patients will be purposively selected to ensure a wide variety of participants defined by gender, age and cardiac status.

The interviewer will audiotape the interviews and will not be an employee of the clinic. The audiotapes will be transcribed and the interviewer will analyse these transcripts. A random set of transcripts will be also be analysed by an independent person to ensure agreement in emerging themes.

How many people will be needed to show this aim?

We will interview patients until no new ideas or opinions are being given in the interviews, and when we have got equal numbers of men/women, those below age 45 and above age 45, and those with confirmed cardiac disease/uncertain diagnosis.

How long will it take?

Month

	0	1	2	3	4	5	6
Recruitment							
Interviews							
Transcription							
Analysis							
Report writing							
Final report							
Submitted							

How much will it cost?

One researcher part-time for six months: £5,000
Transcription costs: £700
Telephone costs: £150
Total: £5,850

Figure 4.2   An example of an outline plan

Resources

All the resources required to complete the evaluation should be estimated and costed – even if they are to come from internal resources. There is always an opportunity cost associated with any activity: what could have been done with the resource had it not been spent in this way? It is best practice to be explicit about the costs of evaluation, which are often underestimated. Going through what will be needed to complete the study may also help to clarify how and by whom the work will be undertaken.

How much will it cost?

Costs are estimated within the plan and need to be explained within any protocol. For example:

Staff costs: one researcher half-time for 7 months = £9,000
Equipment: one computer = £1,000
Printing questionnaires: £600
Travel costs: £200
Total: £8,100

Project management

This is a short statement as to who will be responsible and who will oversee the study. For example:

'The evaluation lead will take overall responsibility for completion of the study, with the researcher co-ordinating and carrying out day-to-day activities. The researcher will report to the evaluation lead. An advisory group will be set up to oversee progress of the evaluation, and to provide specialist advice to the evaluation team. The group will consist of the researcher, a clinical nurse, a patient and the clinical manager. The advisory group will meet every three months.'

Outputs

Finally, the protocol should include a description of what will be produced from the evaluation. This may help to secure external funding, or internal support for the project. Typical outputs may include:

• A final report to commissioners/senior managers
• A lay summary of key findings, for example, for a service newsletter
• A paper to submit to scientific peer-reviewed journal or trade journal
• Presentations
• Training materials.

References

All evidence quoted in the proposal should be supported by a reference to show the source of the evidence (see Chapter 2). We should not make a statement without giving the source of the statement; for example: 'Heart disease is the leading cause of death in the developed world'. We cannot make this statement without showing evidence for this. We could perhaps reference the

World Health Organisation's website, or the British Heart Foundation's annual report, but what we cannot do is just give our opinion without providing any evidence to support it. If it is my opinion that heart disease is the leading cause of death then that does not hold much weight, but if it is backed up by a reference to the WHO or British Heart Foundation then that is much more credible. This also allows interested readers to find out more about the topic, by having the information required to get hold of the original document.

Using our protocol to guide the evaluation

As we carry out our evaluation we need to manage the process, just as with any other project. We can use the protocol to monitor progress, adopting our study timetable to assess whether we are on course or not. During the data collection period of the evaluation, we can use indicators to assess whether we are on target to recruit our sample within the period we have allowed. Indicators are simply points in the evaluation that tell you if everything is going to plan. For example, if we are going to give people a questionnaire, we may decide to record how many are returned from the first 20 given out. This will give us an idea of how long it will take to get 500 back. We can also look to see if the people who reply are representative of the people given the questionnaire (that is, perhaps, only retired people return the questionnaire, and there are none returned from people with young families). Therefore, with appropriate indicators we can see early on if the evaluation is going in the direction we wanted, and if not, then we have time to make changes.

Things do not always go to plan – in fact, they generally do the opposite! This means we need also to consider what to do if things need to change and to have an idea of how to identify when things are going wrong. We may have thought we could look at notes and find the information we want, only to realise early on that the information is not recorded correctly in a large number of cases. We may interview a group of people and then find out there is a different aspect to the treatment which is much more important than that which we are currently evaluating. The plan is an idea of what we want to do, but it can be moulded and changed. However, with a plan we know what we are changing; without a plan, from the beginning there is no clear direction. It is important to agree any changes to the protocol and record them so that the amended protocol remains the guide to the project.

Common pitfalls

Common pitfalls

- **Underestimating how much time and money it will take**. Things do take much longer than most plans anticipate. This can be for many reasons, such as recruitment being slower than anticipated, or because minor things cause delays such as people going on holiday, or our having difficulty organising suitable times to interview patients and doctors. There will generally be costs incurred that have not been considered at the beginning, such as travel to do interviews or to meet people who can give advice on the evaluation, making posters to inform patients about the evaluation, or finding computer programs or books that could help with the evaluation. Building in extra time or extra money 'just in case' is generally worthwhile.

- **Overestimating how much time and help other people are willing or able to give**. For example, when recruiting people in a busy clinic it might seem like a good idea to ask the nurses or receptionist to point out potential patients to take part in the evaluation. However, they are often too busy to make the time and will thesefore forget or they just cannot find the time required. Therefore, we would try not to rely too much on people who are not part of the evaluation and instead would ask colleagues to do as little extra work as possible for our evaluation.
- **Trying to examine too many things at the same time**. An evaluation should really have one or two main questions to answer. It needs to be focused. It may be exciting and interesting to examine lots of different aspects of a clinic being evaluated, but then we run the risk of not getting a clear answer for any of the questions we are asking.

Summary

- A protocol is a detailed outline of what we wish to do, how we intend to go about it and what we hope to achieve. In order to write a protocol we should have a clear background plan.
- We need a plan in order to know what we are aiming to do, to make sure we are collecting the right data, and to be certain we know how we will analyse it, know our budget and know our timescale.
- A plan will make the whole evaluation tighter, more focussed and more likely to deliver something useful that is able to make a difference.
- Planning is a team effort and so should involve and have input from people with different areas of expertise.
- We should visualise each stage of the evaluation and work through it in our heads so that we know the specifics of what will be done.
- The document (that is, our plan) is called a protocol.
- A protocol has some standard sections, such as:

    A title
    A background
    Aims
    Methods
    A timescale
    Costs
    Outputs

- The protocol is our reference document that we refer to as we make the evaluation. We should always try to stick to our protocol, and if we need to make a change we must document and record the change and the reason for the making the change.

Frequently asked questions

If my evaluation is to be undertaken within internal resources, it seems like a waste of time to estimate costs – why should I bother including this in my protocol?

It is tempting to skip this stage, but it is generally good practice to estimate costs so that the time and staff commitment proposed are clear to both the team and your managers. Sometimes it is only when these costs are estimated that it becomes apparent that all plans cannot be carried out, and the costing allows informed decisions to be made about which projects should take priority.

I am planning to take a grounded theory approach to my data analysis, so why should I specify my analysis plans in advance?

When using a qualitative approach based on grounded theory, as with any other approach it is important to be clear about what the research questions are, and how the data will be handled. The method of analysis should still be described, as with any other approach; however, following a grounded theory approach, emerging themes cannot (and should not) be predicted. Instead these should come from the data collected, rather than being imposed.

I would like to involve service users in the planning of our evaluation – how would I go about doing this?

There are various routes that you can use to involve patients, carers and/or service users in your evaluation. There may be a patient representatives' organisation, such as the National Asthma Campaign or Help the Aged, who may be able to help identify someone local to your study. You could also go to your Community Health Council for representation or contact your local Patient Experience Facilitator. You may be able to advertise through a flyer in a clinic, a hospital department or a GP's is surgery.

Whichever way you do it, it is important to understand that the service user may need some support to be able to contribute fully to the group: all their expenses should be met, and they may have some special needs in terms of dietary requirements, mobility/access or the timing of meetings. It may be best to include service users in a different forum to that of the full evaluation team, where the atmosphere can be daunting and the language as well as speed of business inappropriate to lay participants. These things should be considered between the evaluation team and each service user, so that the experience is comfortable for him or her, and in order that their contribution can be effective. However, if a separate forum is used, care needs to be taken that service users' views are not marginalised and treated as less important than the views of professionals and researchers in the overall decision-making processes for the evaluation.

We wish to carry out a local evaluation to look at the impact of our new service on the health of service users – can you advise on how best to go about doing this?

If you wish to measure the impact on health, you need to be sure about the measure you will use and, what size of difference you wish to be able to detect, and then calculate the sample size you will need to include in order to be sure you will have a good chance of detecting such a difference. If you do not include enough people you may miss important effects and conclude there is no benefit, when actually there is an effect and you just missed it! If you don't have the resources to carry out a study that is big enough – or adequately powered – you could take a qualitative approach and accept that you will not be demonstrating impact quantitatively, but rather you will be gaining insight into the range of ways in which individuals are affected by the service – you will get a flavour of the impact from data of this type.

Further reading

Mark Walsh (2001) *Research Made Real: A guide for students*. Cheltenham: Nelson Thornes.

Web pages

www.managementhelp.org/evaluatn/fnl_eval.htm#anchor1577333
www.socialresearchmethods.net/kb/pecycle.php
www.nt.gov.au/health/healthdev/health_promotion/bushbook/volume1/planning.html
www.involve.org.uk/home

5 Research Governance and Ethics

Ethics

Research governance

Research governance is really a set of rules or standards to make sure that research (and therefore evaluation) is of high quality. It is to 'ensure that the public can have confidence in, and benefit from, quality research in health and social care' (*Research Governance Framework for Health and Social Care*, 2005, Department for Health). It ensures that: (1) research is carried out ethically; (2) the research has the design and potential to find out something worthwhile in terms of scientific quality; (3) findings are made public; (4) good clinical practice is followed; and (5) the safety of research participants and research staff is ensured.

It is a code of standards in research covering:

- Ethics
- Science
- Information
- Health and safety
- Finance.

Ethics

Any research that involves patients, health care professionals, organs or tissue, or health data needs to be reviewed by an independent group of people to ensure that it meets ethical standards. This means all health-related research that is doing something new (that is, not doing standard medical practice) needs to be sent to an ethics committee to review. The researchers have to show that they are following a minimum standard of behaviour so as not to harm any participants in the research study.

- The ethics committee will want to see that all the participants are given information about the research and that they have to give their consent to take part in the study *in writing*. If the research is being carried out with people who cannot give their own consent, for example, on young children, people with dementia, babies, people with learning disabilities or people who are unconscious (such as those with head injuries), then the consent of a guardian is needed *in writing*. For example, the parents of children, or the children of people with dementia, or the person's medical doctor in the case where there are no relatives to give consent to the research would be suitable here. This also applies to using tissue samples, where the consent of relatives or the person themselves (if that is possible) is needed before any tissue samples are used in research. For all research, a consent form needs to be completed by all participants.
- All data on patients must be kept confidential and protected. For example, the names and addresses of people taking part in a study should not be kept on a computer that has easy access to the Internet, where others can potentially hack in and download confidential information. The computer should be protected with a firewall and the files containing the information should be password protected. Preferably the computer should be stand-alone and should not be connected to the Internet, with access subject to password protection. Information should not be passed on to others without asking for a patient's consent. For example, if a surgery agrees to take part in a study, they cannot give all the contact details of their patients to external researchers; the surgery would need to contact individual patients and ask their consent to give their notes or contact details to researchers.
- Risks, side effects, pain and discomfort should be kept to the absolute minimum, and any potential benefits must outweigh the potential risks. All risks and side effects or problems need to be clearly explained to patients so that they are able to give informed consent (that is, they must be made aware of the risks and problems and still wish to take part in the evaluation). The information provided to participants is expected to be open and honest. Side effects and benefits cannot be misrepresented. For example, surgery to remove a cancer cannot be said to be a cure with no risks.

Science

The evaluation needs to be made in order to find something new and to not duplicate work that has already been carried out. If there are not enough people in our evaluation to find an answer, then it is a waste of time, money and participants' goodwill to make the evaluation. If other people have examined the problem many

Science of the evaluation has to be strong

times before and we each know the answer already, then it is a waste of time and money to do it again. With resources in short supply, it is not ethical to expose people to treatments or tests or questionnaires if we already have an answer or have not designed the study well enough to give us an answer. Therefore, the science for the evaluation must be strong, and this includes doing a proper background search and planning the evaluation properly to make sure it can answer something new.

Information

The findings from the evaluation should be available to others, so they can learn from the evaluation and benefit from these. This means the findings should not just be presented in a report that is circulated internally, but if it is helpful to other people it should also be made available to patients, health professionals and the general public. If possible it should be published in journals, or placed on posters, or spoken on at conferences and meetings, or given to patients' charities for their newsletters. Even evaluations that are negative and show that something does not work need to published and given to the general public so that other people can learn and not duplicate the evaluation elsewhere when an answer already exists. Negative studies help us to understand what does and does not work and so develop medical services and treatments that are better. When publicising findings we are also presenting our work for critical review so that the methods can be examined by others. This means it is important from the very beginning to plan and undertake high-quality methods and to provide evidence from the findings for every conclusion and recommendation we make. We must be able to justify our findings from the results of the evaluation.

Health and safety

Good clinical practice and proper procedures should always be carried out to protect the health and safety of the staff and patients within an evaluation. If an evaluation requires taking samples, then the disposal of used blood or urine samples should follow standard clinical practice. If a researcher is going to interview a patient, their safety must be considered so that they are not asked to go to a patient's house alone. They should conduct the interview with another person present, or perhaps in a neutral environment such as at a clinic.

The safety of research participants and research staff is ensured

Finance

The evaluation should be designed to be within budget. If it is undertaken and relies on using the resources of a clinic without paying, this could be misuse of public funds. If a person is harmed during the evaluation, then they may be entitled to compensation; the organisation undertaking the evaluation should therefore have the insurance or funding to pay for compensation if required. Expenditure should be planned and accounted for.

In summary: Research governance is a set of rules in the UK (but similar rules exist in other countries) which ensures that research is carried out ethically, using good scientific methods, is made publicly available, follows good clinical practice and health and safety guidelines, and is properly funded.

The ethics process

Before starting an evaluation we need to get research governance approval through the internal processes of the organisation(s) where data collection will take place. In addition, approval from an ethics committee may be required. This is a panel of experts who examine the protocol in order to look at the design of the evaluation to make sure it has good scientific value, protects the participants and researchers, and there is adequate data protection. In the UK the place to start with applying for ethics is COREC (Central Office for Research Ethics Committees), which can be found at www.corec.org.uk

All ethics committees in the UK use the same form and there is a long list of guidelines to follow. The form is at least 52 pages, and we will need to write and submit to the committee the information sheet we are going to give participants (patient information sheet), the consent form we are going to give (a draft consent form is available from the COREC website), the protocol of the evaluation and the CVs of all the people involved in running the evaluation.

There are local committees if an evaluation is only taking place in a local area. There are multi-centred committees if an evaluation is taking place in more than one area, for example in different cities.

When constructing the plan for the evaluation we need to make sure we allow at least two to three months in the time allowed to apply for ethical approval. It can take a number of weeks to get all the paperwork ready to apply for ethics, and then another month for the committee to meet to review an application, and then some more time to make amendments and changes in line with the suggestions of the ethics committee. However, when applying for ethical approval we should prepare all the materials we will need to do the evaluation including, for example, the posters we might put up in the clinic room. Everything we will use must be prepared in advance, and planned and reviewed by independent researchers. This is very useful as we will get the advice and opinions of others, and we will need to think carefully about everything we are doing and plan the evaluation properly. However, applying for ethical approval requires a substantial amount of time, planning and thought. This means if something is not very worthwhile or hasn't been thought through very well, there is absolutely no point in starting it as we will waste a great deal of our own and other people's time.

Basic requirements for ethics

The basic requirements can be found on the checklist that comes with the ethics application pack (this is available in the UK on the COREC website www.corec.org.uk). However, it generally includes:

1. The ethics application form
2. The research protocol
3. The patient information sheet
4. The patient consent form
5. Letters of invitation and poster/advertisement material
6. Evidence of insurance or indemnity
7. A letter from the sponsor
8. A letter from the statistician (if the study is quantitative – that is, based on questionnaires, forms, or databases, and is NOT interview or focus group based research)
9. A letter from the funder
10. Copies of any questionnaire being used or schedule for interviews
11. A summary or diagram of the protocol in non-technical language
12. The CV of the lead applicant/researcher.

From this list we can see that to start to apply for ethical approval, we will need to have a lot of things in place. We will need to have funding to do the evaluation. We will also need a sponsor, that is, an organisation that agrees to take responsibility for the evaluation (normally the employer of the people or person doing the evaluation).

Types of studies needing approval

Ethical approval is needed if you are going to do anything to a patient or person working in a health care system that is different from standard clinical care. Some obvious examples are:

- Giving someone a new drug that has not been licensed.
- Trying a new operation procedure that has not been done before.

Some less obvious examples are:

- Interviewing staff at a clinic regarding their views on a new system. (However, this is changing with the new procedures, so check current requirements from the COREC website before preparing ethical forms.)
- Looking at patients' records to examine if there are any side effects of an existing treatment (see case Study 5.1).
- Allocating patients to two different forms of standard treatment (that is, a broken ankle can be put in plaster or operated on, and both are standard care).

CASE STUDY 5.1

Time to insulin therapy and incidence of hypoglycaemia in patients with latent autoimmune diabetes in adults

Background: Latent autoimmune disease in adults (LADA) is a type 1 diabetes (insulin dependent) which is slowly developing. Patients are not dependent on insulin at onset and therefore are often treated as having type 2 (non-insulin dependent) diabetes. We examined the time to insulin therapy and the incidence of adverse events among LADA patients.

Aims and methods: We examined the patients' primary practitioner records to examine time to initiation of insulin in patients who have LADA compared to those with type 2 diabetes and examined the incidence of episodes of hypoglycaemia in both LADA and type 2 patients.

Results: The median time to insulin for LADA patients (n=60) was two years compared to 10+ years for the type 2 diabetes patients (n=60) (p<0.001). There were 2/30 (7 per cent) cases per year of severe hypoglycaemia among the LADA patients compared to 0/30 (0 per cent) in the type 2 diabetes patients.

Conclusion: Patients with LADA rapidly progress to needing insulin therapy but do not appear to have a high incidence of hypoglycaemia when compared to type 2 patients.

Source: hypothetical example

Question: Why does this study need ethical approval?

The reason why interviewing people will need ethical approval is that in interviewing we might distress people, make them feel pressurised or make them feel their job will be affected by their answers. Therefore, any contact with staff working in a health care setting needs to go through ethical approval. However, if we want to interview members of the community or teachers or people not involved in a health care setting, we would technically not need ethical approval. But, if we work for a health care organisation and that evaluation is for that organisation, then it is very likely that our employer will ask us to apply for approval. This is because an independent review of the evaluation is very useful before starting, and having ethical approval makes everyone more comfortable by showing that the evaluation is 'ethical' and of a good standard.

Patient records are kept for their treatment. If we wish to use them for reasons which are not for standard care (such as evaluating the side effects of different forms of standard care), then we need to apply for approval to do this. We cannot have access to notes and records without a patient's permission. If we want access, we have to apply for approval.

Randomly allocating patients to two different forms of standard care needs ethical approval because we are no longer making a clinical judgement about what treatment a person should be offered. People will be offered treatment based on the protocol of the evaluation. So clinical judgement might be to put in plaster the broken ankle of an elderly person, but the protocol of the evaluation might allocate this person to surgery. Therefore, in order to allocate people to two different forms of standard treatment we will need ethical approval. To decide whether we need ethical approval for a study, the form in

---

Checklist for Researchers

Any research proposal involving human subjects must be submitted for ethical approval unless all the following conditions are met. If there is any doubt then the project should be submitted.

                                                                    YES   NO

- It is true that the project does not affect the treatment or care of the patients involved in the study, nor does it require additional invasive tests or clinical examinations or major interventions.
- It is true that the project does not cause, or is likely to cause, distress to patients or staff.
- The project has the consent of those responsible for the care of the patients and for staff whose workload may be affected by the conduct of the study.
- Information about individual patients/subjects is collected by and only available on need-to-know basis to NHS personnel who are subject to the usual rules of confidentiality.
- If patients themselves are providing information then:

    – consent to be included in the study will be sought by a member of the team currently providing care or a member of the audit team;
    – written consent is needed unless the study only involves the completion and return of a questionnaire;
    – patients will be given information, written wherever possible, about the study including:

        ○ the purpose of the study
        ○ why and how they have been chosen to take part
        ○ what is involved in taking part
        ○ the arrangements for confidentiality of individual information including non-identifiability in any publication
        ○ a statement that participation is entirely voluntary with no changes in their treatment or care or in the attitudes of staff if they **decline** to take part
        ○ where possible and desired, arrangements about the availability of information about the results of the study
        ○ patients must, wherever possible, be informed that at least 24 hours is allowed before they decide whether or not to participate.

IF YOU HAVE TICKED ANY OF THE 'NO' BOXES THEN YOU *WILL* NEED TO SUBMIT YOUR RESEARCH PROJECT TO THE LOCAL RESEARCH ETHICS COMMITTEE

Figure 5.1   Do I need ethical approval?

Source: Provided by the South West Wales Local Research Ethics Committee

Figure 5.1 can help. If we want to work out what type of evaluation we are doing – research, audit or service evaluation – we can use the template from the Central Office for Research Ethics Committees shown in Figure 5.2.

Clinical audit and service evaluations should still adhere to the standards recommended by ethical committees, but the processes for approval are

RESEARCH	CLINICAL AUDIT	SERVICE EVALUATION
The attempt to derive generalisable new knowledge including studies that aim to generate hypotheses as well as studies that aim to test them.	Designed and conducted to produce information to inform the delivery of best care.	Designed and conducted solely to define or judge current care.
Quantitative research – designed to test a hypothesis. Qualitative research – identifies/explores themes following established methodology.	Designed to answer the question 'Does this service reach a predetermined standard?'	Designed to answer the question: 'What standard does this service achieve?'
Addresses clearly defined questions, aims and objectives.	Measures against a standard.	Measures current service without reference to a standard.
Quantitative research – may involve evaluation or comparing interventions, particularly new ones. Qualitative research – usually involves studying how interventions and relationships are experienced.	Involves an intervention to use ONLY. (The choice of treatment is that of the clinician and patient according to guidance, professional standards and/or patient preference.)	Involves an intervention to use ONLY. (The choice of treatment is that of the clinician and patient according to guidance, professional standards and/or patient preference.)
Usually involves collecting data that are additional to those for routine care but may include data collected routinely. May involve treatments, samples or investigations that are additional to routine care.	Usually involves analysis of existing data but may include the administration of a simple interview or questionnaire.	Usually involves analysis of existing data but may include administration of simple interview or questionnaire.
Quantitative research – may involve evaluation or comparing interventions, particularly new ones. Qualitative research – usually involves studying how interventions and relationships are experienced.		
Quantitative research – study design may involve allocating patients to intervention groups. Qualitative research uses a clearly defined sampling frame-work underpinned by conceptual or theoretical justifications.	No allocation to intervention groups: the health care professional and patient have chosen intervention before clinical audit.	No allocation to intervention groups: the health care professional and patient have chosen intervention before service evaluation.
May involve randomisation.	No randomisation.	No randomisation.
RESEARCH REQUIRES ETHICAL APPROVAL.	AUDIT DOES NOT REQUIRE ETHICAL APPROVAL.	SERVICE EVALUATION DOES NOT REQUIRE ETHICAL APPROVAL.

Figure 5.2   Differentiating research, a clinical audit and service evaluation

Source: The Central Office Research Ethics Committees Website
www.corec.org.uk/applicants/help/docs/Audit_or_Research_table.pdf

different. Local structures and processes may vary, but there will often be a committee within an organisation that needs to be contacted before proceeding with a study. We need to ensure that all these processes have been followed. It is possible to cause distress to participants in audit or service evaluation projects, just as in research studies – complaints to the organisation may be made and the study may be put in jeopardy. It is good practice to adhere to the same standards, and to follow internal procedures closely to ensure that any potential harm is minimised.

In summary: Any evaluation in health care may need to have ethical approval. Things which do not require ethical approval are audits (examining if standard guidelines are being followed), service evaluation and evaluations with people who are not part of the health care system. However, if the person doing the evaluation is part of the health care system, then it is very likely that they will be asked to seek ethical approval.

An ethical opinion is always useful because it gives reassurance that the evaluation is of good scientific value (through independent peer review) and is ethically sound. It is possible to contact COREC for an opinion on whether ethical approval will be required for a study being considered, in order to save time, and when the rules are difficult to interpret for a particular proposed project.

Reasons why applications to ethics may be rejected or require amendments

The patient information sheet

One of the most important documents that is sent to the ethics committee is the patient information sheet. This should be a simple description of the evaluation, its aims and what it will involve for those people participating. This sheet should be short and should be understood by everyone. It should be free of technical jargon or complicated medical descriptions. But it also must be accurate and report all the side effects, risks and benefits accurately and realistically. The patient information sheet is frequently one of the documents that needs amendment when submitted for ethical approval. The main reason for amendment is that it is not realistic (namely, it misses some risks or side effects) or is not simple enough to understand. It is always useful to pilot the patient information sheet before sending the final draft to an ethics committee. This means giving the sheet to people who might be like the patients or participants we are hoping to recruit into the evaluation, and asking their opinions and recommendations for changes. The patient information sheet should always be dated and have a version number (for example, Version 3–12/12/07) so that if amendments are made we can always identify the most recent version of the sheet.

Patients' rights are not being protected

For example, if we want to assess data from notes, we may be required to write to all the patients to ask their consent to look in the notes for the purpose of the evaluation. If we want to examine patients' X-rays we will need to ask their consent, even if we look at these when delivering their clinical care. Here we need to ask specifically to look at the medical records/X-rays for the purpose of research. In the same way we may see patients and during the consultation would want to ask them a few extra questions for our evaluation. However, we cannot interview them without telling them about the evaluation and getting their consent to be part of the research. If we apply to an ethics committee to just ask a few extra questions during the consultation without giving patients the information and the choice not to participate, our application is likely to be rejected by the ethics committee.

The scientific value or methods are poor

If the methods have not been planned properly or members of the ethics committee feel there are better ways of doing the evaluation, there may be a rejection. If the question being answered is not helpful or useful in providing new knowledge, it may also be rejected as wasting resources, for example, if we are testing for a condition but our test is inaccurate and not reliable and we do not have a treatment for the condition. Therefore, we will cause worry and stress for those patients given a positive diagnosis (which could be the incorrect diagnosis) and reassure those given a negative result (which may be a false reassurance). This evaluation of a test would not get ethical approval.

Data confidentiality

Data should not be accessible to people outside the evaluation and patients or participants should not be identified outside the study. For example, quotes from participants taking part in an interview should not be identified using the person's name, but should use a number or letter instead. Applications for ethics will be rejected if data protection regulations are not followed. For example, laboratory results should not be e-mailed using the person's name and hospital number as this route is not sufficiently safe for confidential data such as this identifiable, personal and potentially sensitive information.

Consent for children and adults unable to give consent

This applies in particular to people with dementia, head injury, mental illness or learning difficulties. It is often easier to do evaluations or studies just on those people who are able to give consent and can adequately read the information sheets. However, this may be a problem if we are denying vulnerable people the possibility of good treatment, for example, if we want to look at vitamin supplementation to improve the health and risk of falls and fractures in the elderly. We could say that only those people who are capable of understanding the study should be approached. But the people most at risk of poor health and falls and fractures could be those with dementia. Excluding these people would be unethical. Therefore, asking the consent of the nearest relative or carer may be needed. All evaluations using children require the agreement of parents or guardians.

Conflicts of interest

If a study is being done by researchers who would personally benefit from specific findings, then this is a conflict of interest. If a department had substantial funding for staff or equipment from a pharmaceutical company, then finding their drug does not work in an evaluation could be difficult. Therefore, investigators should be under no obligation to find results favouring one direction over another and should not benefit personally from finding for one result over another (that is, no shares in the company producing the product under evaluation).

R&D approval

If the research is taking place in a health care trust, then we will need the approval of that trust. This approval examines if we are using the staff of the health care organisation and if we are compensating the organisation for the use of their staff. For example, if we want someone to pull X-ray records for us, we need to pay for the time taken to find and file these records. If we are asking staff to take blood samples for us, we need to allocate time for the collection of these samples outside of normal clinical hours, so that patients under standard care are not kept waiting or otherwise affected by our evaluation. Every hospital and health care trust will have their own R&D approval forms and should give some support or advice for completing these forms. Often the R&D committee may ask for changes to the protocol or changes to the evaluation, and this means it is often better to get R&D approval before applying for ethical approval as any changes to the protocol need to go back to ethics, although R&D committees will also ask for evidence that the study is being submitted to an ethics committee, and may not give their final approval until the ethical approval is granted.

Applying for approval

An application for approval should follow the steps below, though steps 4 and 5 may have to be undertaken at the same time:

1. Write a protocol
2. Obtain funding
3. Write up all the materials you will need (patient information, advertising material, questionnaires, an interview schedule, input from external advisors such as a statistician)
4. Apply for local R&D approval
5. Apply for ethical approval

It is extremely rare for an ethics committee to come back with absolutely no recommendations for changes or advice. Therefore, an important part of applying for approval is not to take recommendations as criticism but as advice to improve the evaluation. Everyone needs to make some changes to their application – things can always be made better, and if you ask 10 people for their advice you will certainly get some changes, so consider it helpful, not personal.

Summary

- Research governance is a set of standards (in the UK) to ensure that research is of a high quality.
- This code of standards covers *Ethics, Science, Information, Health and Safety, and Finance.*
- *Ethics* ensures that participants in the research are informed and give their consent to be part of the study, that their rights are protected (such as sensitive data are kept confidential and secure), that risks and side effects are kept to a minimum and are outweighed by the benefits gained from the findings of the evaluation.
- *Science* ensures that the design and planned analysis are high quality and correct for answering the questions asked.
- *Information* ensures that the researchers have a plan to tell others about their work, either to give to patient charities or to publish in journals.
- *Health and Safety* ensures that standard clinical practice is followed, for example, patients are always the responsibility of a medically qualified doctor.
- Applying for ethical approval can take a couple of months and this time should be accounted for within the plan of the evaluation.
- Applying for ethical approval will include as a minimum: an application form, a protocol, a patient information sheet, a patient consent form, copies of any material being used, a summary of the protocol and the CV of the lead applicant.
- When applying for ethical approval spend a great deal of time and thought to get the patient information sheet right, try to identify any ethical issues that might be relevant, and ensure that you have had an independent, experienced researcher read your protocol.
- Don't take recommendations for change personally – everyone (even people who sit on ethics committees) needs to make amendments to their application after an ethical review.

Frequently asked questions

I would like to interview patients to find out if their health has improved following the introduction of a new treatment, but I don't have much time to complete the study – do I have to go to through the ethics approval process?

Yes, you do. Unfortunately you should have allowed for this time when you were planning. There is not much point doing the study if you do not have ethical approval as it will go against the guidance for good quality research and so will be hard to publish and will be criticised. If you can't publish it, you cannot tell anyone about your findings, so there was no point starting it. You will take up time and money and will not be able to improve the information and knowledge available on this subject. More importantly, you will be open to being taken to court by patients if they feel your questions were harmful or upsetting in any way, and in a case where you did a study without ethical approval, the patient would rightly win, and you and your employer would need to pay compensation.

My study has been funded through a peer review process – does this mean I can avoid applying for ethical approval?

No, a peer review process helps to ensure that the science is good quality and the funding is being spent wisely. However, it does not look at the ethics of the study. If you are doing new research you need ethical approval.

I would like to apply for ethical approval to do my study – can I get any help with this?

Yes, you can get help from COREC or from the administrators of your local ethics committee. There is a lot of advice on the internet at the COREC website. However, this can take time to find. Most of the help and advice comes from reading lots of guidance notes, which are available on the Internet. Alternatively, you could find someone locally who has previously done an ethical application.

I have been invited to attend an ethics committee to present my study – how should I prepare for the meeting?

If the committee allows you, bring others with you and go as a team. It can be quite daunting to sit in a room with 10–15 people questioning you as it is like a large interview. Different members of the ethics committee will come up with different issues, some of which you might not understand or see what their question is about (especially if you are a bit stressed). So having other people with you to answer some questions can be helpful. Talk to other people before the meeting about what they think of the patient information sheet, and what questions they would have if they were a patient. The patient information sheet is an important part of the ethics process that the committee will look at in detail. Think about the impact your evaluation will have on the local doctors and health care professionals. Many members of the ethics committee are health care professionals and so will look at your study in terms of how it would affect people with their jobs. Put yourself in their position and think about what issues you might have with this evaluation if you were on the ethics committee.

Bring a copy of the ethics application with you so that if they refer to specific items you can look up these items and know what they are talking about. Do dress professionally to give a good image, and stay calm no matter what the questions. The committee are not out to get you (though it can feel like that sometimes) but are just examining the ethical issues in the evaluation. It can be quite stressful, so do think about doing something you enjoy afterwards.

Try to relax and don't jump in with the answers to questions but take time to think and then give a logical answer. If a member of the committee asks about something in paragraph 2 on the patient information sheet, don't guess what he/she is talking about and answer off the top of your head: look up your copy of the patient information sheet and use the time to think logically about your answer. Take the whole committee interview very slowly and give yourself time to think.

I am carrying out a local project to map attendances and analyse patterns across conditions and geographical areas – I do not intend to contact patients or alter treatment – will I need to apply for ethical approval to carry out my study?

This does not sound like a study that needs ethical approval. If you do not identify any individual patients, do not give any identifiers that allow other people to identify patients (for example, pin-pointing a case of a rare condition in a small area can identify an individual very accurately), and you are not changing anything, then this does not need ethical approval. This sounds like a service evaluation.

Web pages
www.dh.gov.uk/PolicyAndGuidance/ResearchAnd
Development/ResearchAndDevelopmentAZ/Research
Governance/fs/en
www.corec.org.uk

6 Collecting Data

Collecting data

We know what question we want to answer. The hard bit is, what is the best way of answering it? There are two broad systems: we could use data that are already available, or we can collect our own new data.

Using existing information

What are existing data? There is a great deal of clinical information collected on patients every day. Theoretically, if we could put all the information in one place we could follow people from birth (hospital records data), through growing up (medical notes held with the general practitioner), to being at school (exam results), in emergencies (emergency records, police records), going shopping (store card databases) and more. With all these data already existing, it seems a waste of time and resources to generate more data if we could use existing data. For health-related evaluation the existing data sources that we are talking about are: medical records, for example, with the primary care practitioner; hospital admission records; out-patient hospital records (such as those held in an emergency department or fracture clinic); records of clinical tests (X-rays, MRI results, laboratory test results, etc); minutes of meetings; and existing audio or video recordings.

The benefits of using existing records are that:

- it is quicker than collecting everything from scratch
- it is a good use of time and resources to utilise what is already there rather than duplicating work
- medical records such as diagnostic tests and hospital admissions data should be accurate and reliable
- we can get answers on large numbers of people
- we can get answers based on everyone in a hospital, so there is no loss of people (when we ask people to complete a questionnaire we will not get everyone responding)
- we can identify and select people with rare conditions or rare events
- the evaluation is less disruptive to people – including patients, practitioners and administrative staff
- evaluation can be carried out more cheaply.

However, the main disadvantages of using routine data are:

- what we want might not be collected
- some data might be inaccurate (for example, ethnic background is rarely entered correctly into hospital admissions databases)
- records are not always complete
- missing records may be the most significant, for example, the case undergoing investigation due to an adverse outcome
- records may be kept but may be difficult to access, for example, stored a long way away, or maybe in transit between where a record was collected and where it will be stored
- the data we want may be confidential and we might not have the right to use them.

Existing records can be used to answer questions about how a system works. Records are collected as a treatment is given and so can give an accurate view of the process and what is happening. (see Case Study 6.1). If data are collected in the same way in different places, for example in various hospitals, then it can be easy to compare local figures with others such as national averages, or averages for the area. For example, time from an accident to hospital or the response time of an ambulance can be taken from existing records and used to compare with other places in the country. Another example would be the use of minutes from meetings which can provide a record of decisions taken in relation to say the staffing of a clinic.

In summary: existing data can give information on very large numbers, quickly and cheaply, with minimal disruption to patients and care providers and in standardised ways so that findings can be compared with others.

Routine data collection: More is not better in the early care of acute myocardial infarction: a prospective cohort analysis of administrative databases

Aims: To assess the outcome and costs of care delivered to patients with acute myocardial infarction (AMI) after initial admission to hospitals with or without catheterisation facilities in Belgium.

Methods and results: From a nationwide hospital register, we obtained the data of 34,961 patients discharged during 1999–2001 with a principal diagnosis of acute myocardial infarction. They were initially admitted to hospitals either (A) without catheterisation facilities, or (B1) with diagnostic, or (B2) interventional catheterisation facilities. Mortality had been recorded till the end of 2003 and re-admissions till the end of 2001.

The chance of death (mortality hazard ratio) at five years in those attending a facility without catheterisation (A) compared (B2) to those with catheterisation 1.01 (0.97, 1.06) (that is, no difference) and for those with diagnostic (B1) compared to those with catheterisation (B2) was 1.03 (0.98, 1.09) (that is, no difference), There was no difference in re-admission rates between A, B1 or B2. The mean cost in hospital of a patient at low risk with a single stay was in A £4,072 (median: 3,861; IQR: 4467–3476), in B1 £5,083 (median: 5153; IQR: 5769–4340), and in B2 £7,741 (median: 7553; IQR: 8211–7298).

Conclusion: Services with catheterisation facilities compared with services without them showed no better health outcomes, but delivered more expensive care.

Source: adapted from Hans Van Brabandt et al., *European Heart Journal*, 2006; 27 (22): 2649–54.

Question: What was done in this study? How were the findings supported?

However, when we use existing records we need to make an assessment of how valid and accurate they are. In some cases the data collected are of very poor quality. For example, there may be a lot of missing data or there is a lot of data which have mistakes, such as dates of birth recorded as 23/23/06. It may also be difficult to understand the data. For example, if the database has a record of two broken arms, is this two broken arms for the same person, the same arm broken in two places, or two different people having broken their arm? In addition, it may be difficult to access the data (for example, much of the data are confidential).

When the data are difficult to use or are of poor quality or simply do not record what we would like to evaluate, then it may be important to collect new data from scratch. However, observing that existing methods to collect data either do not work properly or do not exist is an important finding in itself.

Types of existing data and how to access them

Electronic databases

Electronic databases include, for example, electronic records from emergency departments, hospital admission databases, data from the census or the Office of National Statistics. We can often write to organisations that hold electronic data, such as the Office for National Statistics in the UK, and request data. We need to specify exactly what type of data we need and which fields (for example, date of admission and diagnosis) we want. Often organisations holding the data will not release confidential data such as names and addresses (but they can give area locations) or dates of birth (but they can give ages). We might need to go to hospitals for data such as records from an emergency department or a hospital out-patients, or go to an individual GPs for their electronic records. In this case we need the agreement and approval of the organisation holding the data, such as the hospital or GP practice, and we again need to tell them what fields or which exact data we need. Therefore, access to electronic data is mainly about getting the person who is responsible for the data to agree to give you extracts of the database that they manage.

Clinical notes

Clinical notes would include medical records and notes related to care – ambulance service patient report forms, midwife notes, laboratory results etc. There may be existing records that can be accessed for an evaluation that are routinely gathered and kept, but not in electronic form. It is more time consuming to access these records and to extract data items, but if records exist, practitioners will not be happy to complete the same information in another format for our study. The same confidentiality rules will apply as for electronic records, but it is actually more difficult for hospitals to anonymise these records, so they will need further assurance about the integrity of the evaluators. Records of this type generally hold both structured, 'tick box' type, categorical or continuous data (for example, drugs administered; diagnosis; clinical observations such as blood pressure readings; temperature), as well as some free-text commentary. Data quality can be of concern; some data items may be consistently missing and handwriting can be difficult to read. However, as a direct account of the patient care that was completed at the time of the contact, they can provide a unique source of data about what happened, when and why.

Meeting minutes, existing studies, policies and protocols

Minutes of meetings might be difficult to track down and access, but they can offer a very valuable record of decision making. The best person to start with if you want to trace the minutes of a meeting is the person who chaired it. Some meetings are public meetings, such as a trust's board meetings, and the minutes are publicly available. However, while some meetings are meant to be public meetings it can be a real challenge finding out just where to find the minutes. If the meeting is not a public meeting we need to ensure that we have permission from all the participants at a meeting to analyse the minutes. We also need to ensure that the organisation which hosts the meeting is happy for us to use the minutes as data for the evaluation.

Another source of data can be data from other studies. For example, sometimes a member of the organisation might have carried out a research project as part of a masters' degree and that study can contain information which might be very relevant to your evaluation. If we can be sure of the quality of the work, and the research methods are clearly set out, and the author consents, we may be able to save time and resources by using studies that have already been carried out.

Existing policies and protocols can also be utilised; for example, data might have already been collected about the quality of patient experience as the result of a policy to manage resources more effectively, and if these data already exist and you can obtain consent, then it makes sense to use these in your evaluation.

Video/audio recordings

Sometimes video and audio recordings of events are already in existence. Security cameras video record waiting areas, for example, and these recordings might help with timing people's transit through a clinic. We would need to obtain permission for their use from the organisation which owns the videos, and it is not acceptable to use videos to identify individuals when they have not been collected for that purpose. So timing anonymous patients' transit times would be acceptable. However, identifying bad practice on the part of an individual and identifying a specific nurse or doctor would be rather more difficult, ethically. If we know that an area is routinely recorded for security purposes, it is possible to seek consent from those being recorded to analyse the video recording for evaluation purposes, and if they provide their informed consent it also becomes possible to use the recordings for more in-depth purposes which might well result in the identification of excellent or poor working practices. Some GP training practices routinely video doctor–patient consultations, and it may be possible to use recordings like these for our evaluation. In this case it would be important to seek consent from patients and practitioners in advance of using the recordings. It is not sufficient that patients have agreed that the video can be produced for training purposes if we, as evaluators, are going to use the recording for another purpose. Sometimes it is possible to access existing audio recordings for evaluation purposes, for example, some meetings are tape recorded to allow minutes to be constructed from the tapes. Once again, consent is a sensitive issue and we need to ensure that we do not identify individuals from the tape in a way which could harm them. We also need to ensure that we are sensitive to the need for confidentiality. Sometimes professionals will tape their report on a patient. This is then written up by someone else and sent to another professional and the patient. It might be important to evaluate the way this process is working, but it would be equally important to obtain consent from all the people involved in the process to access the tapes, the letters produced as a result, and the report written up from the tape. Some people can feel that there is a fine line between evaluation and investigation! It's best to keep in mind that the purpose of evaluation is improvement rather than blame.

How to use existing data

First, we need to check if we can have access to the data. Sometimes if we already work in the hospital and do not identify the patient but just use anonymous numbers for people, then access is not a problem. As discussed in Chapter 5, research ethics approval may be required, depending on the nature and purpose
of the evaluation. In addition, we may need permission from the patients or from a patient representative group in order to access the data. The way to check is to find the Caldecott Guardian for the data (in the UK's NHS system). This is a member of NHS staff appointed to protect patient information, and they can be found in each health care trust.

Second, we need to make sure we can understand and interpret the data. This includes understanding the original purpose, processes and systems of gathering the data, and applies to all existing information, including data held on databases. We also need to have or to find someone with the skills to manipulate and interpret the data correctly. This way we can find out more about where the errors or, importantly, any bias might lie.

Finally, once we have accessed and know how to interpret the data, understand the limitations and the possible sources of bias, then we have all we need to do the analysis. This is the good thing about using existing data – it can be quick.

In summary: existing data can be used to evaluate what is actually happening. Existing data can be used to evaluate a system or a process as the data routinely collected can be directly relevant to our evaluation.

Collecting new data

We collect new data when the information we need to answer our evaluation question is not already available. There are several different approaches to the collection of new data, and there are advantages and disadvantages to starting from scratch with new data collection.

Interviews

Qualitative methods are used for gaining an understanding of processes, and perspectives. We know that often programmes don't work the way they are supposed to work, and we need to understand why and how we might improve them. Where interventions are found to work it is important to understand how, why or in what contexts they can be effective. Qualitative methods are very good for this purpose and allow us to ask people who are involved in all aspects of the delivery and receipt of a programme what they think and feel about the programme, its organisation and impact. Researchers cannot always know just which issues are most important to different stakeholders, and researchers may not be able to imagine all the possible impacts of certain ways of doing things. The best way to find out these things is often to ask those involved or to just observe what goes on. So the starting point for qualitative research is to ask, or to watch, listen and learn.

An interview is an interaction between researcher and study participant in which the participant is free to answer questions in their own words. Asking questions can be done in a number of ways, but the most usual way is to ask a series of questions in an interview setting. Interviews can be carried out on a one-to-one basis, or between a researcher and a group of people when they are called focus groups.

The advantage of interviews is that questions can be rephrased and asked in different ways; ideas and themes can be explored and developed as the interview progresses and evolves. However, in this method of collecting information, the interviewer themself can have an effect on the replies given. Therefore, care must be taken in selecting the interviewer to make sure they have the skills and training required in interview technique and that if they are involved in the care or provision of services, or in a hierarchical staff relationship to the person being interviewed, this needs to be taken into account when interpreting findings.

INTERVIEWS

Interviews can be spoken and recorded in some way, including by video or tape recorder, or by notes taken by the person who is carrying out the interview. Interviews can be carried out face to face, by telephone, or by e-mail. While telephone interviews can save time (and therefore money) and some people find them helpful, others may find that it is more useful for establishing the 'rapport' necessary for easy and full communication in a face-to-face situation. There are different ways in which the questions for an interview can be set out.

Structured interviewing: For some studies it might be important to ask all the people being interviewed the same questions in the same order and to stick closely to that format. In this case the answers would not be structured by the interviewer. Respondents should be able to respond with open text, that is, to say or write what they like in response to the questions. But as all are asked the same questions in the same order using the same words, this allows for an easier comparison of the answers. This way of asking questions is often referred to

Structured	Semi-structured
Have you had pain from your new hip?	Tell me how you feel about your new hip.
How would you rate your new hip?	What advice would you give other people about to have a hip operation?

Figure 6.1 Structured and semi-structured interviews

as 'structured interviewing' in the research methods literature (see Figure 6.1). This type of interview is easier for people who are not skilled in interviewing technique. For example, the interviewer may ask 'To what extent does your arthritis interfere with your life?' The interviewer would continue to stick to the listed questions whatever answer is given by the patient.

Semi-structured interviewing: For other studies it is important to be able to follow the lead of the person being interviewed, and just the main topics for the interview will be set out beforehand and some main questions will most likely have been identified. However, the opportunity to follow up new leads that the person being interviewed mentions, or to explore in depth a topic in a way that the researchers might not have thought about is part of these interviews. Researchers can use prompting questions and probing questions to explore new issues in depth. This way of asking questions is often referred to as 'semi-structured interviewing' in the research methods literature. This type of interview is like a conversation and needs to flow from the responses that have previously been given by the respondent. The interviewer might ask 'In what way does your arthritis affect your life?' The next question could then be left to the discretion of the interviewer, and would depend on the answer given by the interviewee, for example, they may then ask 'You talked about the pain of the arthritis, could you tell me a little bit more about this?'

Focus group interviewing: In some studies it is possible to ask a number of people the questions we are interested in at the same time. The researcher can invite people (usually between four and eight works best) to a meeting, which allows them to respond to the same questions as a group of individuals. While there are obvious benefits in terms of time (and therefore money), another benefit can be that people can bounce ideas around with other people, and thus might say more than in a one-to-one interview with a researcher. If we use this approach there may be some problems also. One problem is that people might be uncomfortable describing their experiences in a group – the researcher needs to check things like whether junior staff are combined in the same group as senior staff – which is not a good idea if we want to know how junior staff really feel about the way work is organised! Another problem can be the difficulty of recording and unscrambling who said what and the ways in which different people might have been dominating the proceedings. This way of asking questions is called focus group interviewing in the research methods literature.

Dos and dont's of interview schedule design

Do	Don't
Ask questions as simply and clearly as possible.	Ask long, complicated questions which run two or three issues together.
Ask one question at a time and allow time and/or space for one answer before moving on to the next.	Jump too abruptly from one topic to another.
Ask opening questions which are straightforward and allow people to feel confident about their answers, for example questions about people's personal backgrounds, how long they might have been involved with a service, etc.	Conduct the interview in a public place such as the waiting room where everyone can overhear.
Try out (pilot) your schedule with someone	

Figure 6.2   Interview dos and dont's

In addition to the dos and dont's given in Figure 6.2, these are same practical things to remember when working with interviews and focus groups:

- Tell the participants in advance how long the interview is likely to last.
- Do remember any consent forms, interview schedules (see Figure 6.3) or focus group guides which are needed on the day to share with participants.
- Make sure the interview happens where respondents are happy to talk and can be confident they won't be overheard.
- Allow plenty of time to get to the destination and set up the equipment.
- Identify how to record the responses and test out the technology – if we are planning to tape record a focus group, for example, test the equipment including the microphone in a similar situation to the one we will be using it in.
- If we are using focus groups it is best to have two facilitators – one to ask questions and guide the discussion, one to observe, make notes and operate any necessary recording equipment.

Do offer ground rules for participants; if possible, come to an agreement about confidentiality.

Basics of interviews: The following points should be observed when planning and conducting interviews:

- Develop an interview schedule (see Figure 6.2).
- Bring a tape-recorder, if needed (try it out in advance).
- Organise a place and time for the interview.
- Obtain consent for the interview from the participant.
- Organise a way of having the interviews typed up (transcribed).

The following template is to be used as a guideline to give you an idea of how to prepare your own interview schedule.

Interview schedule for patient's opinion of new tests for diabetes

I. **Opening**

A. (**Establish rapport**) [shake hands] My name is _____ and I am a member of the local health authority.

B. (**Purpose**) I would like to ask you some questions about your views on the extra blood test you had two weeks ago for your diabetes.

C. (**Motivation**) We hope to use this information to help decide if we should introduce this test as a routine test for all newly diagnosed people with diabetes.

D. (**Time line**) The interview should take around 30 minutes.

E. (**Ethics/confidentiality**) Go through written information with participant.

(**Transition**) Let me begin by asking you some questions about what you know about your diabetes following the meeting with your doctor.

II. **Body**

A. (**Topic**) General information about diabetes knowledge.
   (a) Were you given the information sheet?
   (b) What did your doctor tell you?

B. (**Transition to the next topic**) Views of the test.
   (a) How do you feel about the results of the test?
   (b) Would you have the test again?
   (c) Would your recommend others to have the test?

C. (**Transition to the next topic**) Information regarding the test.
   (a) Was the information booklet helpful?
   (b) Did you read it?
   (c) Did it make sense?
   (d) Do you have any questions that the booklet did not answer?

(**Transition**) Well, that is all my questions, do you have any questions?
(**Transition**) Thank you very much for your help and time talking to me about the testing. Let me briefly summarise the information that I have recorded during our interview.

III. **Closing** (I suggest that you put your closing on a separate page so you can allow for room to summarise your interview.)

(**Summarise**)
I appreciate the time you took for this interview. Is there anything else you think would be helpful for me to know?
Thank you very much again for taking the time to help us with this study.

Figure 6.3   Interview schedule

Observing practice

Observation is probably the most expensive approach in terms of time and effort; sometimes it also feels like the most difficult method because it can seem as though a researcher is 'spying' on colleagues or people at work or receiving treatment, therefore invading privacy. One of the most important

Observation

things to remember is that watching for the purposes of evaluation is about learning and understanding what goes on. This approach actually rests on the assumption that researchers do not know everything about everything that occurs and need to understand and learn from participants in any activity.

One way of watching and learning is to sit in on events and make notes or record what one observes with a tape recorder or video recorder. In this situation the watcher tries to limit the impact they have on what they watch, so that things can go on as they would if the researcher was not there. The researcher is observing activity that would happen whether they were there or not, and hoping to gain a better understanding by seeing just what people do in a particular setting. The researcher might make written notes to supplement tape or video recording and will need to spend some time after each watching and listening, eventually writing up these notes. Sometimes researchers can make a kind of chart on which to record the things they see while they are doing their observations – a structured observation.

One benefit of this approach is that researchers can collect a lot of background information while they are doing their observations. The researcher might be able to ask people about particular events at the time of observation and therefore develop a better understanding.

Another benefit is that although people always behave slightly differently when someone is watching what they do, it is also the case that it is better to have information of this type than none at all. This way of watching and learning is called *non-participant or participant observation* in the research methods literature.

Doing observation: We always do a preliminary visit to the site where we will be doing our observation. This can help us identify any potential problems and alert us to opportunities, for instance, is there somewhere to sit where we won't be in the way and interfere too much with what's going on? We need to ensure that we have appropriate permissions to carry out our observation. It is a good idea to dress in a way which doesn't draw attention to ourselves, but shows clearly we are not part of the team being observed.

Covert or overt?:   We need to think about whether we want our observation to be covert or overt – will people know we are observing them? If choosing the covert method, we might decide to watch the people waiting in the waiting room via security cameras, for example. We need to be very sure that we will not breach any of the rules around confidentiality, and to have permission from the organisation. If we decide to observe overtly, then we will need to make arrangements with people beforehand so that they understand just what our purpose is and are happy for us to do the observation. We might need to ask people for their formal consent to observe them, and if we have had to apply for permission from an ethics committee we are likely to have to ask people to sign a written consent form which we will have prepared beforehand. It is good practice to obtain written consent in all cases where we are observing individual interactions. This needs to be done before we begin our observation, and we need to think about what we will do if people do not wish to be observed. It is often a good idea to send people information about the fact that they might be observed at a clinic, for example, in advance of the actual clinic so that they can decide about whether they are willing to be observed or not without feeling pressurised in any way. We always provide a contact number if we send out information in advance so that people can contact us with any queries they might have about the project.

Capturing data: Before capturing data we need to plan what data we want to record and how we will do this. It is possible to make field notes where we try to record the most relevant things for our evaluation aims. Or we might decide that we want to devise a chart or schedule beforehand to capture relevant events. It is also possible to video record or tape record interactions if all parties are willing. These methods provide us with a much more complete record of what goes on, but we then face the task of transcribing tapes or video tapes before we can begin our analysis.

We have to remember that our purpose is to observe what would go on if we were not present, so we need to be as neutral as possible. We mustn't be tempted to join in the interaction, as this might change what we want to observe.

We need to be careful about practical matters such as the length of time we are likely to be observing; if possible don't plan to observe anything without a break for more than a couple of hours. It is not possible to pay proper attention for longer periods and we are likely to miss valuable details. Observation is actually quite physically tiring!

We need to make sure we take all the materials we are likely to need with us, for example, spare copies of any chart or schedule and plenty of tapes and spare batteries if we are tape recording. Always test the tape recorder before beginning a session and always ensure the microphone is switched on!

In summary: When observing practice we need to record the relevant details about the events that are specifically related to our evaluation aims.

Questionnaires

We can ask interview-style questions in writing. We can ask people face to face to write answers to our questions. One advantage of this written approach is that in some circumstances people might be more comfortable with writing answers in their own time. Their answers can be kept anonymous. In these circumstances there is a bit of a grey area as to what is an interview and what is a questionnaire. Some questionnaires can be delivered face to face, some interviews can be written. If we wanted to make a distinction, we would say that in an interview the answer we record and analyse is the full text from the respondent. However, questionnaires have fixed answers.

What is a questionnaire? Questionnaires are generally a set of structured questions that all the participants are asked. Generally they are given to people to fill out themselves. However, for children or people who are not able to complete a questionnaire, they can be completed face to face.

The benefits of using a questionnaire are:

- We can reach a large number of people (for example, postal questionnaires).
- It is structured, so we can ask everyone the same questions and so easily compare participants' answers. This means we get a focused answer to specific questions.
- It is consistent, making it easy to extract the data for analysis. We can get standard answers from identical questions, so interpretation is much easier.
- If we make the questionnaire anonymous we can ask questions that might be sensitive or are on topics that a person might not talk about in a face-to-face interview situation.

Therefore, they provide a cost-effective way of getting new knowledge on a large number of people. They are most useful if we want to ask fairly straightforward questions and feel that standardized responses will give us all the information we require.

Problems with questionnaires are:

- People have to agree to fill out a questionnaire and so we will miss some people if they do not complete the questionnaire.
- We may miss information because we only allow limited answers.
- There might be a lengthy time involved in developing the questionnaire, publishing it, distributing it to participants, getting the replies back, putting the replies on a computer and finally analysing the data.
- Not everyone may be able to fill out a questionnaire. For example, one study using a questionnaire design to follow up people with a hand injury had a very poor response rate, and of those who responded most had gone back to work and were better very quickly. This is because the people with hand injuries could not complete the questionnaire– only those participants with very minor injuries were able to complete the form. There can be a variety of problems associated with completing questionnaires: people may be too young to do so (children), or they may have reading and writing difficulties due to illiteracy, old age or medical reasons (arthritis, eye conditions), or the language of a questionnaire may not be written in a person's first language.

Steps in designing a questionnaire: There are huge numbers of existing questionnaires to look at complex issues like depression, quality of life, and the impact of medical conditions on work. A list is given in Figure 6.4. If we are interested in looking at the impact of disease on function, well-being, relationships with others, or other complex issues, then we should take a look at what is already published. There is no point re-inventing the wheel when there are plenty of existing questionnaires to choose from, from the disease specific to the generic (can be used in any disease). This is where a good literature search will help us identify what other people have used and what are the best questionnaires in this area. Published questionnaires will have already been tested on a sample of patients and shown to be valid, that is, that they are repeatable, reliable, sensitive to change, and measure what they report to measure. Existing questionnaires can be used to measure things that are not one-offs, but things 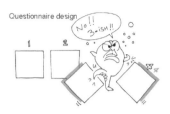 that we will measure repeatedly and that other people might wish to measure in their local area. Using previously validated and published questionnaires allows us to compare our findings with those of other studies, so this can help with setting our evaluation in context with other places. We can incorporate existing questionnaires into new questionnaires we are developing. So, for example, if we wanted to look at the impact of injury on quality of life, we might ask our own questions about the injury but then supplement these with an existing quality of life questionnaire. This will help us address our specific issues in addition to providing the validity described above.

Name	Description	Reference
SF36	A quality of life measure which looks at 36 items related to quality of life.	J. Ware and C. Sherbourne (1992) The MOS 36-item short-form health survey (SF-36). I. Conceptual framework and item selection. *Medical Care*, 30: 173–83.
EQ5D/EQ6D	A quality of life measure which looks at five aspects of quality of life.	J. A. Johnson, et al. (1998) Valuation of EuroQOL (EQ-5D) health states in an adult US sample. *Pharmacoeconomics*, 13: 421–433. http://gs1.q4matics.com/Euroqo PublishWeb/
Beck's Depression Inventory	The BDI is a self-administered 21-item self-report scale measuring supposed manifestations of depression. The BDI takes approximately 10 minutes to complete.	www.swin.edu.au/victims/ resources/assessment/affect/ bdi.html
HAQ: Health assessment questionnaire	The HAQ was developed as a measure of outcome in patients with a wide variety of rheumatic diseases. It has also been applied to patients with HIV/AIDS and in studies of normal aging. Its focus is on self-reported patient-oriented outcome measures, rather than process measures.	http://aramis.stanford.edu/HAQ. html

Figure 6.4   Existing questionnaires measuring complex issues

Before developing the questionnaire we need to do some careful planning. We need to really think what data we need to get from the questionnaire. We need to build in enough time to pilot the questionnaire and make amendments before sending out the final version. We need time to send out reminders for people who do not respond the first time, and time to enter the data and analyse the results.

Deciding the questions and answers: Sometimes before even beginning to think about the questionnaire, we need to be sure we understand the questions. For example, if we were interested in examining well-being for people with arthritis (Case Study 6.2), a pilot study/focus group can help to identify the main issues which need to be included in the questionnaire, and to identify appropriate language to use in questions for that particular group. Focus groups or interview methods can be used to identify the range of answers to include for all the questions. In most questionnaires there is a limited set of possible answers that the respondent can give. However, these can be decided or designed based on findings from more open qualitative research methods such as focus groups or interviews.

CASE STUDY 6.2

Development of a questionnaire

The Bath Ankylosing Spondylitis Patient Global Score (BAS-G)

We report on the design and validation of a global measure (the Bath Ankylosing Spondylitis Patient Global Score, BAS-G) which reflects the effect of ankylosing spondylitis on the patient's well-being.

A pilot study was performed to select the most appropriate wording for BAS-G. Then using 392 patients with AS, BAS-G's construct and predictive validity and test-retest reliability were assessed. Correlations between BAS-G (global well-being score) and disease activity and function were calculated. The distribution of the responses covered the whole scale. As predicted, BAS-G correlated best with disease activity ($r = 0.73$), followed by function ($r = 0.54$). Predictive validity was satisfactory: there was an improvement (mean = 29 per cent) in in-patient BAS-G scores over a two week treatment period ($P < 0.001$). Test-retest reliability was excellent (one week $r = 0.84$, 6 months $r = 0.93$). BAS-G correlates well with both BASDAI and BASFI, suggesting that disease activity and functional ability play a major role in patients' well-being. The score is sensitive to change, reliable, and meets face, predictive and construct validity criteria.

Source: adapted from S. Garrett (1996) *British Journal of Rheumatology*, 35 (1): 66–71.

Question: How did the researchers write the questionnaire (design the questionnaire)? How did the researchers validate the questionnaire?

Delivery of the questionnaire: We need to decide on the broad approach of the questionnaire, such as: is it self-completed by the participant or is it completed by an interviewer in a face-to-face situation using an interview style questionnaire? Will all the questions be closed with only a selection of pre-set answers, or will there be open questions which allow people to write a paragraph of text that we need to analyse?

With a questionnaire given face to face or by telephone: using a structured interview, we can include people who could not otherwise complete a written questionnaire (children, the elderly, people with eye or hand injuries, and people who cannot read or write in English). Face-to-face delivery of the questionnaire allows interaction to take place on complex or unclear issues, and allows for probing and verification. We can use more complex questions in our questionnaire because the interviewer is there to clarify the question. However, this style of questionnaire delivery is more costly and time consuming. If we are talking about sensitive issues, then it may not be appropriate as the respondent may not want to talk to a stranger about these issues. Alternatively, telephone questionnaires can have many of the advantages of face-to-face questionnaires, as well as being less costly and therefore more people including in the evaluation for the same resources. However, it does mean that participants have to have a telephone and cannot be hard of hearing.

Handing out or posting questionnaires to participants is the most common and most cost-effective way of getting focused and structured replies from participants. These questionnaires can reach a large number of people and can be used for sensitive topics due to the ability to provide anonymity. However, questions have to be fairly simple as there is no opportunity to clarify them, it is very difficult to examine complex issues using set questionnaires, and there is no opportunity to change the sequence of questions. It can be very easy to bin self-completed questionnaires or to miss entire questions in the questionnaire. Finally, we cannot actually be sure that the person we intended the questionnaire for is the one who filled it out.

Dos and dont's questionnaire design: There are many dos and dont's to observe when designing a questionnaire (see Figure 6.5). Therefore, it should be direct, short, simple and easy on the eye. When you first look at the questionnaire in Figure 6.6 (even without reading the questions), how do you feel about it? The questionnaire should be simple and precise, only asking questions that are essential to the evaluation. It should also be focused, with a clear relevance to the topic being evaluated. The questions should be designed with a definite vision of the essential issues and what the researcher is going to do with the data. For example, if we ask people to tick their age category (such as 15–20, 21–25, 26–30), this means we will not be able to work out mean ages and compare average ages among different groups. See Figure 6.7 for the types of questions that can be used in questionnaires.

Do	Don't
Use simple language.	Use acronyms, abbreviations, jargon and technical terms.
Keep the questions short (less than 20 words) and specific.	Use vague or ambiguous questions, for example, 'Do you eat cheese frequently?' – what is frequent to me might not be frequent to you. Other vague words that are open to interpretation include 'commonly', 'usually', 'many', 'some' and 'hardly ever'.
Keep the questionnaire short. Only ask questions on issues directly relevant to the evaluation.	Use double-barrelled questions such as 'Do you find your doctor friendly and knowledgeable?' as these will contain two separate questions that might have separate answers.
Give clear and easy-to-follow instructions.	Write a great long paragraph of text that describes what responders need to do, as this will be confusing and irritating to the participants.
Make the questions clear and easy, with no room for interpretation.	Use words that have different meanings for different people, for example, 'dinner' can be lunch or tea.
Make the questionnaire attractive and easy to read. Use big text, organise and set it out well so it does not look dense and confused.	Use any questions that could be offensive or annoying or upsetting to people.
Pilot the questionnaire to see how long it takes to fill in and if any questions are difficult to understand, and also identify any problems.	Use repetitive questions, such as asking date of birth and age when one can be calculated from the other.
Make sure there is a stamped addressed envelope, or at least clear instructions of how to return the completed questionnaire.	Forget to include a paragraph explaining what we are using the questionnaire for so that the participant can see the value of the evaluation, what the results will be used for and who might benefit from this work.
Start with general questions first, such as name, age, sex, time since diagnosis. The participant should feel comfortable with the questionnaire and find it simple and easy to complete from the beginning.	Start with specific questions such as 'Please tick symptoms of your bowel disease: diarrhoea, blood in stools, gas, stomach cramps.'
Make the task of filling out the questionnaire as straightforward and simple as possible.	Ask questions that most people will have to complete as 'Not applicable' or 'Don't know'. The participants should be able to complete the questionnaire.
Weed out repetitive questions so that you are not asking the same question twice using different words.	Ask leading questions like 'Would you agree that doctors need to spend more time with patients?'
Make sure you have sufficient options in the answer, and do have an 'other (please specify)' option.	Make presumptions. For example, asking 'How many people live in your house?' This can be annoying if the respondent lives in a care home (the elderly or children) or in temporary accommodation.
Pay attention to the way questions are numbered.	Just put in questions without thinking about how you will analyse the responses. We need to consider how we will analyse these as we write the questionnaire.

Figure 6.5   Questionnaire dos and dont's

Hospital _____ Date _____ DOB: _____

Name: _____ Age _____

1. Where does the child or young person live?

House Name/Number _____

Street: _____

Town _____

Postcode _____

2. Was the child or young person's injury caused by:

Accident   ☐   Deliberate violence   ☐   Unknown   ☐

3. Where did the accident happen?

	Playground	
	Corridor, hall, dinning room	
At school/educational establishment	PE/Gym	
	Classroom	
	Other	
In work	Voluntary	10+ hours per week
		5–10 hours per week
		1–5 hours per week
	Paid	10+ hours per week
		5–10 hours per week
		1–5 hours per week
At home	Own	Other
		Garden
		Bathroom
		Stairs
		Kitchen
	Residential	Other
		Garden
		Bathroom
		Stairs
		Kitchen
Leisure	Entertainment areas	Pub
		Café
		Cinema/bowling
		Skate park
		Public playground
	Countryside	Open land
		Beach
		Sea
		Forestry
	Sports	Field games
		Tennis court
		Cycle/race track
		Swimming pool
	Public roads	Pavement
		Public roads
		Cycle path
		In a car/bus
Other		
Unknown		

Figure 6.6   Example of a poorly designed questionnaire – how NOT to present a questionnaire

1. Yes/No answer

Example: Are you currently in pain now?   Yes   No

2. Agree/Disagree

Example: Would you agree or disagree with the following statement? The main symptom of arthritis is pain.   Agree   Disagree

3. Choose from a list
Example: Which ONE of the following is the most important symptom of your arthritis?

Pain   Tenderness   Discomfort
Fatigue   Swelling   Stiffness

3. Statement

Example: Please describe the quality of the pain you experience due to your arthritis.

_____

_____

_____

4. A list

Example: Please list the most important symptoms of your arthritis.

1. _____   4. _____
2. _____   5. _____
3. _____   6. _____

5. Scale

Example: Please mark on the line below the overall level of pain you have experienced in the past 24 hours.

0 _____ 10

6. Rate items

Example: How significant are the following symptoms for you?

	Not significant				Very significant
Pain	1	2	3	4	5
Fatigue	1	2	3	4	5
Tenderness	1	2	3	4	5

Figure 6.7   Types of questions used in questionnaires

Other methods

Patient diaries: One method used in evaluations like cost/benefit evaluations is to ask
patients to keep a diary. For example, we might
ask a patient to keep a diary or log of all the
medication they have taken or the other medical products they have used so that a value can
be put on the cost of having a condition. We
might also ask them to keep a diary of any side
effects and problems they have experienced
using a new drug. As with all research methods,
the use of a diary has to be carefully planned to

Ask patients to keep a diary

fit the purpose for which it is intended. Importantly, it has to be simple to
use and simple to complete. It should be quite quick to complete as people
are unlikely to want to spend a long time each day filling out their diary. It
should also ask for something to be completed quite regularly. If something
is quite rare, then there is no need asking someone to keep a diary as we can
ask them at the next clinical visit. Diaries should instead be used for common but perhaps minor events – events that might be forgotten between
clinical visits, such as falls (a falls diary for an elderly person) or episodes of
stomach pain (starting a new drug). When designing the diary it is important to think about how we are going to analyse it. It might be nice to ask
people to write a paragraph each day on how they feel using a new drug, but
how are we going to analyse it? We need to think about some structure for
the diary. If we want to know about side effects and the number of episodes
of nausea, then we need to ask people to complete a list of side effects every
day. We need clear labels and numbers, such as:

Side effect: Nausea
Days affected: 3

Introducing new tests: In some evaluations we want to collect data that
involve additional procedures, such as blood tests or other clinical tests
that are not routinely carried out within a clinic. Often at the planning stage
it may seem very easy to just add an extra blood test when a patient is having routine bloods done. However, adding extra tests is often not that simple. Just to take an extra tube of blood the patient requires to consent to the
extra blood test. This means they have to be given information about the
test and what the results will be used for, who will get the result and how
the result will impact on their treatment. Giving the information and getting
consent can be time consuming. People running a routine clinic often do not
have the time to tell people about a test and get their consent, so generally
this part needs to have been done beforehand. This means that adding a
new test, as with everything else in research, needs to be planned and
piloted. Everyone has to be happy to make extra time for new tests. If we do

not have the agreement and backing of the individuals being asked to undertake the work of doing the test (for example, the nurse, the laboratory, and others), then it will not work. Few people will be given the test, therefore any results will not be reliable and perhaps blood samples will be left on the side as laboratory staff do not know what is to be done with them when they arrive. Even the simplest, additional test needs to have the consent and backing of all the staff who will be involved.

Data collection specific to evaluation of costs

Collecting data related to costs will often include the use of existing routine data, questionnaires and patient diaries. When collecting the data we might need to examine costs from different perspectives - that of the patient, the health system, and/or that of society. The conventional way is to classify costs into one of three categories.

First, there are the direct costs, which can be sub-divided into the direct health care costs, the costs to other agencies resulting from a health care provision, and the direct costs to patients and their families. These result from the time patients allocate to the receipt of health care services and the costs incurred in having to travel to and from health care facilities thereby incurring other expenses, such as over-the-counter medication, purchasing equipment and aids to ease the burden of a condition. In addition, it includes the time individuals devote to caring for relatives and friends, in conjunction with or in place of the formal care agencies.

Second, there are the indirect costs or productivity costs associated with health care. These occur outside the health care sector and relate to losses of production, due to absenteeism and reduced productivity, plus those incurred through the informal care process – either as a result of a carer giving up paid employment or by sacrificing their leisure time to provide care, which would otherwise have been provided by formal care agencies. In terms of work losses, the term 'productivity costs' is now used, and this refers to the costs associated with a lost or impaired ability to work, or to engage in leisure activities due to morbidity or lost economic productivity due to death (Phillips, 2005).

It is the intangibles which provide the biggest headache in terms of measurement and valuation but in essence they provide the biggest distinction between health care and other commodities. These are things which by their very nature can be identified, but also have to be experienced in order to be measured and valued.

We need to quantify as many of these as possible and then translate them into a monetary measure using appropriate cost values. These can be derived from many existing sources, such as the British National Formulary (BNF), which gives the cost of medicines in the UK; the National Labour Statistics (National Statistics New Earnings Survey, www.statistics.gov.uk) which can be used to estimate the cost of loss of work; the National Schedule of Reference costs (www.dh.gov.uk/en/Publicationsandstatistics/Publications/

Publications PolicyAndGuidance/DH_4070195) which can be used to identify the costs to the health system; and the Unit Costs of Health and Social Care (www.pssru.ac.uk/pdf/uc/uc2006/uc2006.pdf) which are also helpful. This is where talking to a health economist is vital, as there are many public sources of cost estimates that can be used to inform an evaluation. For example, the cost of arthritis (see Case Study 6.2) might be:

Use per average patient per year

In-patient care	1.6 days	£698
Day cases	0.6 days	£48
Consultations	2.5 visits	£216
Other health care	8.1 visits	£387
Medication		£154
Loss of work capacity	20 per cent early retirement	£3,183
	10 per cent reduced working hours	£654
Total cost		£5,340

This estimate of the cost of arthritis can be used to inform the health care system and can also be used to estimate the true cost of drugs. Using the example of a new drug costing £10,000 per year being released, if this drug allows people to stay in work, stops other forms of medication and reduces visits to hospital, is it worth it? Based on the current estimate above, it is not worth it; overall, it would cost more to treat people with the new drug than to continue with existing treatments. But economics is not only about costs. It is also concerned with the costs and benefits associated with treatments. The question that needs to be asked is 'Are we prepared to pay the additional costs to secure the additional benefits?' For example, if the new drug greatly improves quality of life and generates additional QALYs (quality adjusted life years) at a reasonable additional cost, then it will represent value for money. We would need to examine quality of life (using a quality of life questionnaire such as the EQ5D or the SF36; see Figure 6.4) for those taking the new drug compared to those not taking the drug. Therefore, in order to conduct an economic evaluation we would require the collection of patient diaries to record visits to health professionals, medication use, time off work, and the use of home helps or caring relatives. We can use questionnaires to record longer-term, less frequent events such as investments (for example, modifications to a car due to disability) or surgery. We can also use routine data, such as emergency department records, admissions to hospital or out-patient clinics and the public sources of cost estimates. Thus, a cost-effectiveness evaluation can be quite complex, and specific books dealing with just this topic are available (some references are given at the end of the chapter). However, this book is not aimed at conducting health economics evaluations and we would recommend that anyone undertaking this type of evaluation should access those books specifically aimed at this topic.

Validity of the data

When collecting data, any type of data, it is important that the data are valid. Valid data reflect what they report to reflect, and it should be consistent and accurate (see Chapter 3). There are often many sources for the same data, for example, to find out when key symptoms began it is possible to look in a patient's medical notes and to ask them directly. Different sources of the same data can be brought together to be used to show that the data are valid and reliable (that is, they reflect what they are supposed to be measuring and give constant results). This is called 'triangulation by data sources'. Whether the findings can be generalised or whether they truly represent the programme we are evaluating is determined by the sample of people chosen. Therefore, all data, whatever way they are collected, need to be:

- Reliable (Do we get the same answer if we use the same method with the same person at a later time, does a different researcher get the same answer if they use the same method?)
- Valid (Is the measure we are using a good reflection of what we are trying to show?)
- Representative (Do the people we have sampled represent the group for whom this evaluation applies?)

When we analyse qualitative data we are concerned to show that our claims are based on what the data show us, and that as far as possible we have collected data that represent a reliable picture of what is going on. We can do this by being very clear about what our methods were for collecting the data, thus providing transparency of process. We can also do it by attempting to reduce researcher bias, that is, the tendency to shape data in favour of one position or another depending on what we already believe. For example, wherever possible it is better not to have those people who have delivered a service to a patient asking them questions about their satisfaction with the service. It is easy to see here that the patient might be uncomfortable with telling the person who provided a service that they were not happy with what was provided. Another way we can ensure that our interpretations of data are reliable is to get more than one person to interpret the data, and then to check with each other that we are happy that the interpretation really does represent the data. This is 'inter-rater reliability' (see Chapter 3).

Summary

We can collect data using:

- Existing data (routinely collected clinical or operational data).
- New data collection

  – Interviews/focus groups/observing practice
  – Questionnaires/diaries/new tests.

- Data collected should always be reliable, valid and representative.

Frequently asked questions

If I am running a focus group and everything gets out of hand and goes wrong, with everyone starting to fight and argue – what do I do?

It is important that there are two people facilitating a focus group – one person to ask the questions and ensure that everyone has a chance to make a contribution, and one to record the answers with the tape recorder and observe what is going on. It is also important to establish ground rules at the outset so that everyone agrees that they will respect everyone's right to make an equal contribution without being interrupted or treated rudely. Having established the ground rules it is important to stick to them so that as soon as someone interrupts the first time, the facilitator can remind people of the need to be courteous and head off trouble. If it is clear that, for some reason, people are not prepared to abide by the ground rules, it is best to halt the focus group, switch off the tape and have a short discussion with the participants about whether it will be possible to continue. One more try might result in success, but as soon as people move away from the ground rules for a second time and don't heed a reminder, it is best to cancel the group and attempt to reconvene another group. It is not appropriate for a focus group to become a battleground over an issue, although it is possible for people to have strong opinions, and everyone should as a result be able to express themself without any fear.

Should I do interviews in the patient's own home?

It can be necessary to interview patients at home, and some patients prefer to be interviewed away from the site of their care. All researchers should take the same precautions that anyone visiting a stranger's home would take in the course of their work. For example, always tell someone where you are going, how long you expect it to take and what time you will return, or alternatively check in by phone. If you feel insecure or anxious about a particular interview, you should discuss your worries with a supervisor or colleague and decide whether you want to be accompanied at the interview – although this might be seen as an extra burden for the person you are interviewing. Also remember that you might need to take batteries for your tape recorder as there may not be a convenient power source, and always allow plenty of time to find the address.

If I can't understand the person I am interviewing at all, their accent and what their answers mean, should I just keep going and rely on the tape?

This is a matter for your own judgment. Obviously the person you are interviewing might be upset or offended if you suddenly cancel the interview – it is important if you do halt the interview to present the problem as one which you are experiencing rather than one which the person you are interviewing has caused. On the whole, if at all possible it is best to continue the interview and attempt to decipher the tape later.

I have been observing practice and have seen practice that I think is totally wrong and I am worried about – can I interfere?

This is a difficult ethical problem and will depend on the severity of the practice and your role in the organisation. If patients are being harmed, then you have a responsibility to speak up on their behalf and should describe your concerns to a senior member of staff. This should be included in the participant information sheet as part of your 'contract' with them – that you would report instances of practice that could be potentially harmful and inform them in this instance.

I could use records that already exist for my study, but one or two additional data items would be useful – shall I design a new form for practitioners to fill out for patients who are suitable for my study?

The answer depends on how useful the new items are. Unless the additional items are really essential it would be best to use the existing data only. If we start collecting new items of data, then we are more likely to need ethical approval, plus the time and money to develop and pilot the new form, and we will need to take up the practitioner's time filling in the form and our own time recording these answers. If we have the time, money and the agreement from the practitioners and the new items add a lot, then it is worth collecting new data. However, if the items do not add too much more to our evaluation, then we really should not burden other people (with completing the form) and waste money developing and entering data that are not very useful.

I do not want to jeopardise the anonymity of participants in my study, so how do I send out reminder letters and questionnaires to people who do not return their first questionnaires?

This is a bit more complicated, but basically we need two people or a barcoding system. The easiest way is with two people. Put a number on each stamped addressed return envelope. This number corresponds to where the questionnaire was sent. When an envelope comes back this number is recorded by one person and the unopened envelope is given to a second person to open and record information from the questionnaire. After a specific period of time, numbers which have not sent a questionnaire back are automatically sent another questionnaire to the same address. This way, the person who knows the addresses does not know the responses and the person who knows the responses does not know addresses. No one then knows whose questionnaire belongs to which address, and we can send out reminders to those who have not replied. A better but more expensive way is to have a bar code on the return envelope. This is scanned on arrival and so a computer system can be set up to send reminders without the researcher knowing the addresses or identities of respondents.

If I make sure I get enough questionnaires back to meet my target, why should I worry about the ones who do not take part, or who do not respond?

The ones who do not respond may be very different from those who do respond. For example, if we do a questionnaire study to follow up people who have had an injury, we may exclude those with more severe eye and hand injuries, children and some frail, older people. We might also have excluded some very important groups of people as those with hand injuries and eye injuries may be the most affected in their daily life, and children and elderly people are more likely to have injuries. We might meet our target with lots of people who have DIY injuries to the foot, but is this representative of injuries in general?

I plan to use a questionnaire that has already been validated as a tool for measuring quality of life in a general population – can I assume it will work for my patient group, who have been seriously injured?

No, questionnaires should be used in the population in which they were validated. We need to find a questionnaire that has been validated in a seriously injured population or else validate this questionnaire ourselves in a seriously injured population.

I measured how many times older people in my sample fell during the study period in two ways – by self-report questionnaire and through medical records – so how do I know which data source is more accurate?

They are both different and accurate. Self-report is likely to pick up minor falls and medical records are likely to pick up more serious falls. We would expect that any falls resulting in a hospital admission or a visit to the medical practitioner would be recorded in the self-report. If they are not, then we might question the validity of the self-report. However, we would expect a person might have a number of minor falls and these would not be recorded in the medical records as they did not need to visit a doctor. We might use the two sources to either validate the self-reported falls or to record all falls by combining both sources to identify severe and minor falls.

Further reading

J. Brannen (2007) 'Working qualitatively and quantitatively', in C. Seale, G. Gobo, J.F. Gubrium and D. Silverman (eds), *Qualitative Research Practice*. London: Sage.

M. Drummond, B. O'Brien, G. Stoddart, and G. Torrance (2005) *Methods for the Economic Evaluation of Health Care Programmes*, 3rd edn. Oxford: Oxford University Press.

M.J. Kelly (2007) 'Qualitative evaluation practice', in C. Seale, G. Gobo, J.F. Gubrium and D. Silverman (eds), *Qualitative Research Practice*. London: Sage.

A.N. Oppenheim (1992) *Questionnaire Design, Interviewing and Attitude Measurement*, 2nd edn. London: Pinter.

C. Phillips (2005) *Health Economics: An introduction for health professionals*. London: Blackwell/BMJ Books.

L. Prior (2007) 'Analysing documents', in C. Seale, G. Gobo, J.F. Gubrium and D. Silverman (eds), *Qualitative Research Practice*. London: Sage.

Qualidata (1998) *Legal and Ethical Issues in Interviewing*. Qualidata website www.qualidata.essex.ac.uk

D. Silverman (2000) *Doing Qualitative Research: A practical handbook*. London: Sage.

7 Understanding Numerical Data

We have collected a lot of data – questionnaires, medical notes and results of laboratory tests – but how do we set about using them? The first step is understanding our data.

There are two types of data, quantitative and qualitative. *Quantitative* data deal with quantities or numbers, and include any data that we collect that we want to quantify to get a percentage, proportion or score. Quantitative data can be used to summarise or bring all the data together, to provide one 'average' answer. *Qualitative* data might give a description, while quantitative data can give a single answer, like 2.4 (s.d. 0.5). However, this summary answer is only useful if we understand what it means.

We need to understand about numbers in order to analyse our data and interpret our findings.

The basic ideas of working with numbers

Variation
In all data there is natural variation. For instance, some people are tall, some are short and most are of average height. If we find that there are differences in the average height of two groups of people, this could be due to the natural variation that occurs, and there just happen to be more of the

taller people in one group, that is, this is a 'chance' finding. It could, however, reflect a real difference between the groups, related to who is in the group, for example, more men in one group, different ethnic groups and so on. If we have very large groups any difference is more likely to be a real difference – as we include more and more people, very tall or very short people will have less effect on the overall average for the group – and there will be many more average sized people in each group.

When we want to measure the impact of a new service or treatment, we need to understand whether any of the differences found, for example, between waiting times before the service was introduced and waiting times after the service was introduced, are likely to be due to natural variation in waiting times, or may be related to the introduction of the new service. The answer to this will depend on several things: how much natural variation there is in waiting times; how many records were included; and the size of the difference found.

Going back to the height example – if we find that most children born of vegetarian parents are shorter than those born to non-vegetarian parents, is this just a chance finding? Is the difference between the height of the children caused by a natural variation in height among all children, or does a vegetarian diet affect growth? The answer depends on:

- how much height variation there is in the children of vegetarian and non-vegetarian parents
- how well the average height of each sample (sample of children of vegetarian parents and sample of children of non-vegetarian parents) really is a good reflection of that group overall
- how big the difference is in average height of the groups.

Therefore, understanding the data is really about understanding if a finding is due to chance (natural variation in people) or if a real difference is due to a treatment.

Samples

When we do an evaluation we want to report on a group of people, called our population. For example (see Case Study 7.1), our population could be people registered with mental health services. We can never contact all those people registered with mental health services, so we will have to take a sample. When we do take a sample we need to be sure that we have a group of people who are representative of the whole population. We need to make sure that our sample does not just include, for example, younger people or more males as compared to the population. We want, in the end, to look at the data from our sample and generalise these to the whole population. So our sample has to be generalisable and representative of the population (that is, the population who are registered with mental health services).

Because of natural variation and chance, every sample will give slightly different results and this must be taken into account when we interpret the data. This is called sample variation and lies at the heart of understanding the data.

The REACT study: randomised evaluation of assertive community treatment in North London

Objective: To compare outcomes of care from assertive community treatment teams with care by community mental health teams for people with serious mental illnesses.

Design: Non-blind, randomised, controlled trial.

Setting: Two inner-London boroughs.

Participants: 251 men and women under the care of adult secondary mental health services with recent high use of in-patient care and difficulties engaging with community services.

Interventions: Treatment from assertive community treatment team (127 participants) or continuation of care from community mental health team (124 participants).

Main outcome measures: Primary outcome was in-patient bed use 18 months after randomisation. Secondary outcomes included symptoms, social function, client satisfaction, and engagement with services.

Results: No significant differences were found in in-patient bed use (median difference 1, 95 per cent confidence interval – 16 to 38) or in clinical or social outcomes for the two treatment groups. Clients who received care from the assertive community treatment team seemed better engaged (adapted homeless engagement acceptance schedule: difference in means 1.1 (95 per cent CI)), and those who agreed to be interviewed were more satisfied with services (adapted client satisfaction questionnaire: difference in means 7.14 (95 per cent CI)).

Conclusions: Community mental health teams are able to support people with serious mental illnesses as effectively as assertive community treatment teams, but assertive community treatment may be better at engaging clients and may lead to greater satisfaction with services.

Source: adapted from H. Kilaspy et al., *British Medical Journal*, 2006, 332 (7545): 815–20.

Question: The study reports patients 'were more satisfied with services' for patients receiving care from the assertive community treatment team (compared to continuation team). The difference in means was 7.14 (95 per cent CI: 0.9 to 13.4). What is the interpretation of this statistic?

Data

Discrete data

The type of data determines what we can do with these. Data can be:

- **'nominal', 'name' or 'categorical'** for example, drugs (such as aspirin, codeine, and paracetamol). We cannot divide these data, or multiply them, but we can work out their proportions. For example, 50 per cent of people took paracetamol for a headache.
- **ordered or on a scale**, for example, data about pain could be made up of categories describing its severity: severe pain, moderate pain, mild pain. Again, we cannot multiply and divide these data, but we can give order or rank to the data. For example, people with mild pain have less pain than those with severe pain (we cannot rank nominal data such as aspirin, codeine and paracetamol). This type of data is called ordinal data (ordered data).
- **related**, that is, through measurements, such as height or weight where data are related to each other and so a reading of two is half of four and double one. These are called ratio or continuous data. It is possible to multiply or divide these measurements and make ratios (someone aged 25 is half the age of someone aged 50), making them very useful for analysis.

It is important to understand these properties of data, so that we can plan our data collection to best fit the analysis we would like to carry out. For example, if we want information about people's ages, we can either ask people their age or ask people their age category (that is, 21–25, 26–30, 31–35 and so on). If we ask people their age we would have ratio data. We can work out an average or 'mean' age. We can divide and multiply and work out the youngest and oldest (maximum and minimum ages). We can compare the mean age between groups to see if there are any differences between groups. If, however, we ask people for their age category we can only say, for example, 50 per cent of this group were in age category 26–30. But we cannot work out maximum or minimum ages. We cannot work out a mean age, and it is much more difficult to compare ages between groups. The analysis we can carry out with ordinal data (categories) is limited. Therefore, we need to think in advance about what we want to do with our data. This determines what type of data we collect. The type of data we collect determines the methods of analysis and ultimately the interpretation of the findings.

Frequency curves

With any type of data we can look at how often we find particular characteristics or events in our groups – this is called frequency of occurrence. For example, we can look at the number of red, blue or orange Smarties in a tube (Figure 7.1) or the number of people with different injury severity scores (Figure 7.2). Both of these examples are using nominal (categorical)

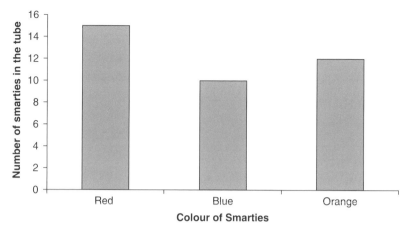

Figure 7.1   Number of Smarties in my tube

Severity of injury using Injury Severity Score

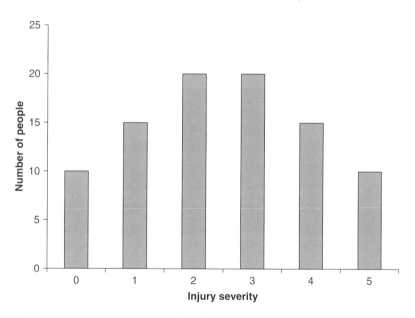

Figure 7.2   **Number of people with different severity scores using the Injury Severity Score (a system assigning a discrete score based on threat to life and other factors related to injury severity)**

data – sometimes called 'discrete variables'. This means we either have red or blue but cannot have reddish-bluish, mid-red/blue Smarties. We can have a severity score of one or two but we cannot have one and a half severity. We cannot have any scores between our groups. Discrete variables mean we have one thing or another, but we cannot have anything in the middle. Although data of this type can be drawn on a graph or pie

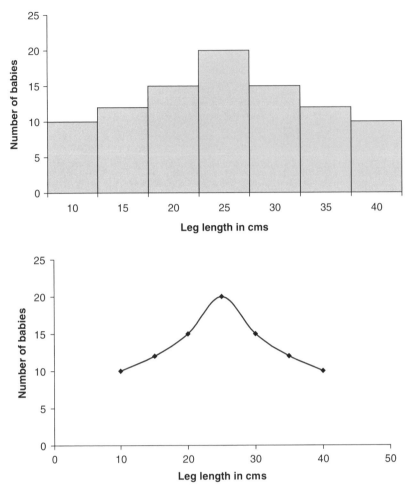

**Figure 7.3   Frequency distribution of leg length in newborn babies shown as a
bar chart and frequency curve**

chart, we cannot draw a continuous line between points, as it makes no
sense.

If, on the other hand, we have collected ratio data (continuous data), then
it is possible to find any number between a range of points (for example, a
person can be aged 25, 26 or any point in between). If we have continuous
data, then we can plot a frequency curve (Figure 7.3).

To make a frequency curve, we draw a bar chart with no gaps between the
bars (called a histogram) to show that this is continuous and not discrete
data, and we can plot a line between the mid-point of the bars to make a frequency curve. We can only make a frequency curve with continuous data. In
Figure 7.2 we cannot join the mid-points of the bars, because these are discrete data. There is no continuation between scores 1 and 2. However, we
can make a curve joining the bars of continuous data, as you can have a leg
length between 20 and 25 cms.

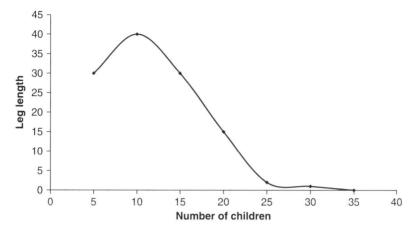

Figure 7.4   Leg length in premature, newborn babies

Normal distribution

With continuous data, if we get a curve that looks like Figure 7.3, then this is called a normal distribution. That is, there are greater numbers in the middle and smaller numbers at the ends. In nature most continuous things have this type of distribution, for example, the weight of babies. There will be an average weight, with some babies naturally being smaller and some babies being bigger. If our data are normally distributed, then there are certain tests and analysis we can do with the data. If the data are not normally distributed or are discrete data, then we need to do a different set of tests. Data that are not normally distributed might look like Figure 7.4. These data are referred to as skewed, and we cannot do certain tests with these data.

Measures of average

A frequency distribution gives a general picture of the spread of the data. However, with most analysis we will just want to find two measurements, one indicating the average and the other indicating the spread of values around this average.

- The average value for ratio data is usually calculated using the mean. This is simply where we add up all the values and divide by the total number of values. In Figure 7.3 the mean (average) leg length would be 25 cms.
- The average for ordered data is the median. This is where we line all the values up in order of smallest to largest and then find the value in the middle of this ordered line of data. In Figure 7.2 the median (average) would be a score of 2.5.
- The average for nominal or name data is the mode. This is the most frequent value. In Figure 7.1 the mode (average) is red Smarties.

However:

- we can use the mode for any data, as we can give the most frequent age or weight or most frequent severity score.
- we can use the median for ordered or ratio data, as we can order age, weight and other ratio data (we cannot put in order nominal data such as Smartie colour, as we cannot give an order to Smartie colour. We cannot say red is less than blue or divide red with blue to work out the value in the middle).
- the mean can only be used for ratio data as we cannot add up and divide nominal (Smartie colour) or ordinal data (severity of injury).

We can see, then, that with continuous or ratio data we have the most options about the analysis and presentation of findings.

Measures of variation

It is important to understand variation in data, so that we can carry out the most appropriate analysis and understand our findings. If there is a wide, natural variation in data, then we may need to include more patients, as it would be more likely to have difference between groups by chance. The simplest measure of variation is the range: this is the difference between the largest and smallest values. The problem with this is that it is based only on two of the observations, and the larger the sample then the larger the range tends to be, as we pick up the more extreme and odd observations in larger samples.

A better indication of the variation in data is given by the standard deviation. This is the average deviation (distance) from the mean. It is worked out by subtracting all the individual observations from the mean, adding them together minus one, and then dividing by the number of observations.

Standard deviation is particularly useful if data are normally distributed. With all data that are normally distributed, 70 per cent of all observations will lie within one standard deviation of the mean, and 95 per cent will lie within two standard deviations from the mean. So this means that:

If the average leg length of newborn babies is 25cm (standard deviation = 5cms), then:

(25 + 5 = 30 cm AND 25 − 5 = 20 cm)

70 per cent of the babies in our sample had a leg length of between 20cms–30cms.

95 per cent had a leg length of 15cm–35cm.

(See the understanding numbers programme to practise this and also examine the measures of variation that are associated with the mode and median.)

To recap: There are three types of data:

1. **Name (nominal) data**: The most frequent value is called the mode. This is the way we measure the average value when we have nominal data, for example, the painkiller most often used is paracetamol.
2. **Ordered (ordinal) data**: To work out the average value we line all the observations up in order of least to most and pick the value in the middle. This is called the median, for example, the average severity of an injury is a score of 3 on the injury severity scale.

3. **Ratio or related data**: To work out the average we add all the values up and divide by the number in the sample. This is called the mean. We can work out how good the mean is at giving a true reflection of the data by working out the standard deviation. That is, we take each observation and subtract it from the mean and then we work out the average deviation. In any sample, one standard deviation above or below the mean tells us the range where 70 per cent of data lie, and two standard deviations above and below the mean tell us the range where 95 per cent of the data lie.

Sampling variation

When we do a study, we usually do not include all possible people, but instead select a sample (see Chapter 3). We take a sample of the population in order to draw conclusions about the population from our findings in the sample. For example, if we study a small group of people registered with mental health providers (Case Study 7.1) this could be in order to talk about service provision for all people registered with mental health providers. However, if we took three separate samples it is likely that these three samples will have slightly different means and standard deviations. This difference is due to natural variation in the individuals within the different samples. This is called sampling variation.

   If we collect many different samples and calculate the mean of each one of them, we can work out the most frequent mean (which mean occurs in most samples). The most frequent mean would be our best guess of the population mean. For example, if we wanted to know the average weight of all newborn babies in the UK we could access the hospital records for 20 different hospitals in the UK. We could put all 20 means together and get the mean of all these means. We could then work out the standard deviation of all these means. This would tell us the most likely population mean (average size of babies in the UK). It would give us an estimate of the weight range where 70 per cent of babies should lie and the weight range where 95 per cent of babies should lie. Using this information can help us to understand when an observed weight is unusually high or low, perhaps indicating an underlying problem. For example, we can tell when a baby is abnormally big (perhaps the mother had diabetes) or abnormally small (therefore the baby needs to be monitored for growth). Unusual values can be simply the result of natural variation, or could be a cause for concern.

In summary:

- Every sample will be slightly different.
- The average of some samples (the mean) will not be near the true population mean. This is due to natural variation.
- The average of most samples should be around the true population mean.
- If we know the standard deviation of lots of samples we can estimate what our population might look like (that is, what the average value is and the ranges where most data should be).

The standard error of the mean

If we have lots of samples and we work out the standard deviation of all these samples, this is called the *standard error of the mean*. With this standard error of the mean we can estimate how close our sample mean is to the true population mean. For example, if we have a lot of samples of babies' birth weights, and the averages of these samples are really very different, there will be a large standard error. This means that there is a lot of variation in baby weight. In this case, estimating the average for the whole population from just one small sample will be hard because there is a great deal of natural variation. Therefore, if we know the standard error of the mean, then we can say how close the average in our one sample is to the whole population mean.

How good is our sample at predicting the population mean? We can work out the standard error of the mean using just one sample. To do this we can look at the standard deviation within the sample and the number of people (or observations) in the whole sample. The standard error of the mean is worked out by dividing the standard deviation of our sample by the square root of the number in our sample.

As with standard deviation, we can work out standard errors by adding one standard error to the mean to tell us where we are 70 per cent sure our population mean might lie, and we can add two standard errors to the mean to tell us where we are 95 per cent sure that the population might lie. For example, if we do one sample of 50 babies' weights and the mean weight is 3.65 kg, the standard deviation is 1.0 and the standard error is 0.14. This means we think that the average baby weighs 3.65 kg, that 70 per cent of babies will weigh between 3.51kg (mean – standard error of the mean) and 3.79 kg (mean + standard error of the mean), and 95 per cent of babies will weigh between 3.37 (mean – 2 standard errors) and 3.93 kg (mean + two standard errors). We can also express this in a different way: we can be 70 per cent sure (or confident) that the true population baby weight is between 3.51 and 3.79 kg, and 95 per cent sure (or confident) that the true population baby weight is between 3.37 and 3.93 kg. (Please see Figure 7.5 for an example of this.)

Why do we need to know about the standard error of the mean? Understanding the errors of the data we have gathered is important for their interpretation. Often we will take one sample and say that this reflects the whole population. However, we should always report the standard error as this tells us by how much our estimate might be wrong.

95 per cent confidence interval

This brings us to something else that is very similar, called *95 per cent confidence interval*. If we compare two things (weight of babies born in winter compared to weight of babies born in summer) we will find a difference between the two things: average baby weight in winter = 3 kg; average baby weight in summer = 3.5 kg. This tells us the difference in our SAMPLE. However, what might the difference be in our POPULATION? We can work out the 95 per cent range for the *difference* in our samples, and this is called the 95 per cent confidence interval. So, for example:

Example (Nominal data): A pack of playing cards represents our population. In a pack of cards there are:

26 red cards – 13 hearts and 13 diamonds
26 black cards – 13 clubs and 13 spades

(a) **We are allowed to sample three cards. We get two spades and one club.**
We believe our whole pack consists of black cards, 66 per cent of them are spades and 33 per cent are clubs. We estimate our population is black and predominantly spades.

(b) **We are allowed to sample ten cards. We get two hearts, one diamond, four clubs and three spades.**
We believe our pack consists of red and black cards, 30 per cent are red and 70 per cent are black. The majority are clubs (40 per cent), then spades (30 per cent), then hearts (20 per cent), then diamonds (10 per cent).

(c) **We are allowed to sample 25 cards. We get seven hearts, six diamonds, seven spades and five clubs.**
We believe our pack consists of red and black cards, 48 per cent are red and 52 per cent are black. The majority are hearts (28 per cent), and spades (28 per cent), then diamonds (24 per cent) and clubs (20 per cent).

In conclusion: The more we sample, the closer the estimate is to the real population (or real pack of cards).

Example (ratio data):

I want to find the average birth weight in the hospital. The true average birth rate in the hospital is 3.5 kg.

I look at the birth weights of five babies born on one night of the year. The mean is 3.4, the standard deviation is 1.2 and the standard error is 0.5.

Therefore I think that the population mean should be between two standard errors or 3.4 +0.5 and 3.4–0.5 = 2.9 kg – 3.9 kg.

Even with my small sample size I did get quite close to the true population mean, but there is quite a large range in the standard errors.

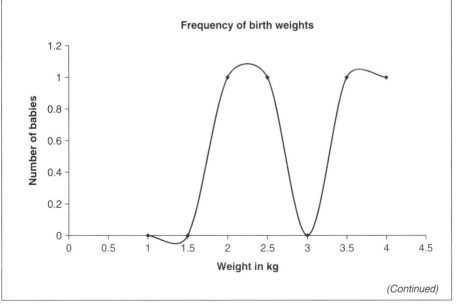

Frequency of birth weights

(Continued)

(Continued)

I sample 50 babies born over one week in the hospital. The mean is 3.65, the standard deviation is 1.0 and the standard error is 0.14. Therefore, the mean should lie between 3.51 kg – 3.79 kg. This is a much more accurate estimate of the population mean.

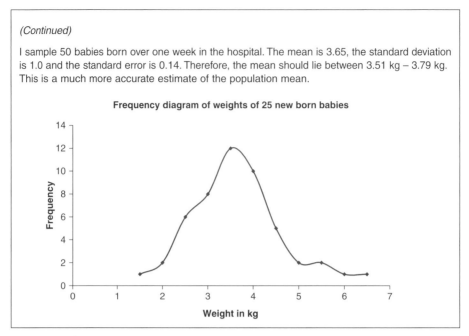

Figure 7.5   Sampling

We know the babies born in winter in our sample are 3 kg. The standard error might be 0.25 kg, so in the population we are 95 per cent confident the average winter baby is between 2.5 kg and 3.5 kg.

We know the babies born in summer in our sample are 3.5 kg. The standard error might be 0.25kg, so we are 95 per cent confident that the population average summer baby is between 3 kg and 4 kg.

Our difference in weights of babies in our sample was:
Summer weight minus winter weight or
3.5–3.0 = 0.5kg

However, in our population the difference might be as little as:
Summer weight minus winter weight
3–3.5 = –0.5 kg (winter baby weighs more)

And as much as:
4–2.5 = 1.5 kg (summer baby weighs more)

So although in our sample the summer baby weighed more, in the population the difference might be the other way round (winter baby weighs more) or as much as 1.5 kg different. So our comparison showed that the difference was 0.5 kg but the 95 per cent confidence interval for the population was between –0.5 kg and 1.5 kg. So in the population we cannot believe there is a real difference in babies' weights between summer and winter.

In summary: Standard deviation says how much natural variation there is in our SAMPLE. Standard error says how close our sample average is to the

POPULATION average. The 95 per cent confidence interval tells us the difference that we might expect in the POPULATION when comparing the two things.

Sampling

We have discussed sampling in terms of designing the evaluation. However, we also need to consider it in terms of interpreting the data. As we discussed in Chapter 3, the main reason for sampling is that it is often not feasible to examine all of the population, and so we must take a sample. This is why we have specific sampling strategies and can develop a sampling frame (a list of all the people eligible to participate in the evaluation). We can undertake random, quota or systematic sampling in order to get a group of participants that are representative of the population. However, we have to remember that any sample is at risk of sampling error and bias. We may design a good evaluation with a good sampling frame and sampling strategy, but we also need to examine the data we get in the end to  make sure our sample is representative. For example, we need to look at the participants who did not respond to our invitation or questionnaire. We need to compare the characteristics – such as age, sex, ethnic group–of these non-responders with those who did respond. This will make sure we have not missed a whole group of people in our sample. We also need to look at the people who initially participated but then dropped out or were lost (for example, they moved away or died) before our evaluation ended. If we do not account for the participants who were lost during the evaluation, then our end findings could be biased and inaccurate (as we are perhaps missing an important group of people such as those who were so ill that they died, or those participants who were not benefiting from a programme, for example for weight loss, and who therefore stopped attending).

Thus, we not only need to consider what our sample will look like in the design, but we also have to examine it when we are interpreting the data. Could the result we have be due to any type of bias?

Sample size

An essential part of any evaluation is deciding how many participants are needed. Including too many is a waste of resources and participants' time, and including too few will mean we might not be able to answer the questions we aim to address in the evaluation. We need to do this for both quantitative and qualitative studies. However, we have to do this in different ways for each type of study. Working out the sample size for a quantitative study is not always very straightforward, but there are some essential steps.

In a study where we are looking to find a difference between groups – for example, those who received the new service and those who did not – to work out a sample size, we need to know what differences we want to see and work out how many people will be needed to see these. So to work out a sample size for this type of study, we need to know the following.

What differences are we expecting?   For example, if we want to

show that taking aspirin reduces pain more than just drinking water, the first step is to think about how much of a reduction in pain we are interested in. We can set our sample size at the number that we can be fairly confident will allow us to detect a difference in this size – a smaller difference may be missed, and it is important that we understand

Sample size is not always very straightforward

this at the outset. If, say, participants are asked to rate their level of pain from 0–10, we might say that we are interested in detecting a reduction of 3 (on a 0–10 scale) – that this is the minimum difference that will be important to people, and that we expect those in the aspirin group to report an average reduction of 3, while for those in the water group we expect no change. We might suggest that reducing pain by 1 on a 0–10 scale is really not very useful, and the participant probably would not feel that much better. However, with a reduction in pain of 3 on a 0–10 scale, the participant might feel quite a lot better. This is called the clinically relevant difference. A clinically relevant difference is a change that would be useful and relevant to patients if it occurred. Therefore, we can work out how many people we will need in the study to find a difference of 3 (on a 0–10 scale) between the aspirin group and the water group. If, however, aspirin actually only reduces pain on average by 2 (on a 0–10 scale), then with our sample we may miss this difference and conclude that aspirin does not reduce pain any more than water. In this case, we would draw our conclusion based on our initial decision that a reduction of 2 in pain score is not clinically meaningful. There are many studies, however, where the sample size is not formally worked out at the outset of the study, and false conclusions are drawn about effectiveness because not enough people are included in the sample to detect important effects. This would be referred to as an 'underpowered' study. We could say that there is no effect for a treatment, when in fact there is an effect but we have not had enough patients in the study to show it.

However, many evaluations are not set up to look at just one thing, but rather to look at a range of different things. In this case, we can identify the most important question (the primary question) and work out our sample size based on making sure we include enough people to be able to answer that question. If we do this we have to be aware that we may not be able to answer all of our other questions confidently with the sample we include. So we can work out which question is likely to need the most number of participants and calculate the sample size on this question. In general, the smaller the difference we want to be able to detect, the larger the sample we need.

To estimate how often something occurs in a population, we can also use a sample and generalise from our findings in the sample. Again, the bigger the sample we use, the more confidence we can have that the rate we find is close to the true (population) rate. We need to think about how accurate our estimate needs to be, and work out what sample size we will need to be confident of being within, say, plus or minus 5 per cent of the true rate.

Another issue is that often we don't know what differences there will be before we do a study. For this we can do a pilot study and look at any variation we find in a small sample, then use this information to estimate what we may see in a larger sample.

What is the variation in the population?   The number of people we need depends on how much natural variation there is in the population. This will tell us the size of the sampling error we might see. Therefore, we need to know the standard deviation that is likely in the samples we are going to get. But if we have not done the study yet, how do we know the standard deviation? We can look at other people's studies and see their standard deviation, we can look at routine data and see the standard deviations among patients, we can do a pilot study or we can just recruit a few people and work out their standard deviations. However, if we just estimate it from a few patients, then it would be useful to re-calculate the sample size when we have more participants and are a little way into the evaluation. This will give us a better estimate of the standard deviation, and therefore the number of people we would need to aim to include.

What errors will we accept?   When generalising findings from a sample to a population, there is always a risk of making errors due to bias or the play of chance. We can minimise these risks, but need to understand the level of risk we are willing to accept. Generally, the bigger the sample, the lower the risk of error. If we pick a sample that is too small, we will not be able find a difference even if one exists. Our evaluation will lack the power to detect a difference. The bigger the study, the more power it has to detect a difference (for example, the difference in pain relief due to aspirin *vs.* water).

But the bigger the study the more it costs and the longer it takes, so we have to work out the minimum number of people we can recruit and still have the power to find a difference. It is standard practice to accept a power of 80 per cent, which means we have an 80 per cent chance of finding a difference if one exists. In some cases we might think this is too low and would wish for a 90 per cent chance of finding a difference. If this is the case, we will need to recruit more participants. Therefore, when calculating sample size we need to know what level of chance (of missing a real difference if one exists) we are willing to accept. The smaller the study, the bigger the risk is that we will miss a true effect.

If we do find a difference between groups (for example, the aspirin group had more pain relief compared to the water group), we then need to think about what level of risk we are willing to accept of this being an error. If we find a difference there is always the chance that this is due to natural variation in samples. That, although we have found a difference in our sample, in the real world (the population) there is actually no difference. This can happen because our samples are small groups with lots of variation and so there may appear to be a difference, but this is indeed an error. Standard practice is to accept a 5 per cent risk that any difference we find is actually by mistake, due to sampling error. When we report our findings, we can say that a difference has been found at the significance level of 0.05 (5 per cent). If in particular cases it is important to be more sure of any difference, we can set the significance level that we report at 1 per cent, meaning that there is only a 1 per cent chance that the difference is due to chance and the finding is actually an error (significance level of 0.01 or 1 per cent), and then we need to take a larger sample. Understanding significance or p-values is very important in interpreting findings. (For an example of this look at Case Study 7.2.)

CASE STUDY 7.2

A pilot study for an emergency department-based organ donor card centre

Objective: This study was done to examine attitudes concerning an emergency department-based organ donation enrolment programme and whether such a programme would be good for targeting under-represented groups.

Methods: A total of 300 non-acutely ill patients attending the emergency department was asked to complete a survey: 290 completed the survey and ten refused. Chi-squared and independent T-tests were performed on categorical and continuous data respectively.

Results: Ninety per cent (261/290) were interested in organdonation information through the emergency department. The likelihood of currently holding a donor card was affected by age and race (p = 0.049 and p = 0.001 respectively) but unaffected by gender, income, being head of the household, and the number of people or age of people living in the household. Sixty per cent (60/100) who did not already have a donor card were African-American, but 71 per cent (43/60) would be willing obtain a donor card from the emergency department.

Conclusion: An emergency department organ donation recruitment programme would be acceptable to patients and would be an effective way of recruiting people who do not currently have a donor card.

Source: adapted from D. Cheng, P. Ku and B. Brenner (2005), 1 abstract published in *The European Society for Emergency Medicine*, 1–5 September, 286.

Question: In this study the authors have examined age, race, gender, income, head of household, number of people in household and age of people in household, and have found both age and race significant. What is wrong with this outcome?

To work out sample size in practice, please do go through the self-taught 'understanding numbers' course that accompanies this book.

In summary: To work out sample size we need to know: (1) what difference are we expecting; (2) what is the natural variation in the data; (3) what is the chance we will take that we will miss a real difference (less risk needs larger sample); and (4) what is the chance we will take that if we find a difference that it is really due to natural variation (lower risk needs larger sample)?

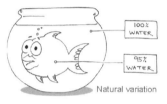

Summary

In understanding data we need to know that:

- In data there is natural variation.
- There are three types of data (nominal, ordinal, ratio), which require different analysis techniques.
- Different samples will have different averages due to natural variation.
- Generally, natural variation will mean that most of the data will be around an average value, with fewer and fewer occurring as we move outwards from the average. This is called the normal distribution of data.
- If data are normally distributed, then 50 per cent of the data will be above the average and 50 per cent will be below the average.
- 95 per cent of the data will be between two standard deviations above and below the average.
- We can estimate the average of a population from one sample. We can then use the standard error of the mean to estimate how close the average from our sample is to the average of the population.
- We can work out how many people we need in our sample by knowing the difference we need to find, the amount of natural variation in the sample, and the error levels (missing a difference and falsely finding a difference) we are willing to accept.

Frequently asked questions

If I plan to present my findings grouped by age, should I collect actual age or is it OK just to ask participants to tick a box with an age range?

If we decide to collect age ranges there is very little we can do with the data. We will have reduced our data to normative or name data. We cannot work out a maximum or minimum age, and we cannot work out a mean or median age or range. Instead, all we can say is that 35 per cent of people were in the age range of 25–45 (for example). Therefore that is it – we cannot say much more. If we ask for actual age we can compare groups for average age, report the youngest and oldest, work out any deviation, and so get an idea of how all the ages are distributed. We can manipulate the data much more if we ask for actual age. So if at all possible we should aim at the highest level of data (ratio) and not aim at the lowest (nominal).

Can I use some data that we collected last year for another study to calculate the sample size for this next one?

Yes, provided they come from the same population and are examining the same measures. So if last year's study was on patients attending a clinic and this year's study is also on patients attending a clinic, then there is no problem.

My sample size calculation says that I should include 5,000 people in my study, but I don't have the resources to carry out a study of that size – what should I do?

Generally, the best thing to do is to rethink what you are investigating. Develop aims that are achievable within the resources. You might need to set your sights a bit lower. There is no point starting an evaluation if you know from the outset that you do not have enough people in the study to find an answer. It is just a waste of time and resources.

If this is the aim that you must evaluate, then the alternatives are to seek more resources or to collaborate with someone else who is doing a similar thing and then combine your findings in the end. So perhaps you can recruit 2,000 people and they can recruit 3,000, and therefore by working in a combined way you can achieve the sample size needed. This is used in many big and well-funded studies.

However, if you have limited resources, the best thing to do is to rethink your aims.

I worked out my sample size on the primary question that the Steering Group advised was most important, but since then another of the questions has become the most important – what should I do?

There are a few alternatives:

1. Carry on as before and answer the question you set out answer. You can report on findings on one of the other questions, but your study was not designed to answer this question and so is not placed to come up with a definitive answer on this topic.
2. Carry out a sample size calculation to work out if you are recruiting enough people to answer the question (then you need to think about whether you are collecting data in the right way to answer this question). If it is feasible to address the question, then you can report on an answer, but you do need to acknowledge in the discussion that you have amended your protocol and have not done the evaluation as planned in the beginning, and then explain why this change has occurred.
3. Stop the study you are doing (if it is still early enough) and start from scratch to design the evaluation around the new question.

Further reading

B. Kirkwood (1996) *Essentials of Medical Statistics.* London: Blackwell Science.

B. Kirkwood and J. Sterne (2003) *Medical Statistics.* London: Blackwell Science.

Web pages

www.bmj.com/statsbk/
www.bmj.com/cgi/content/full/315/7104/364
www-users.york.ac.uk/~mb55/pubs/pbstnote.htm

8 Storing Data

Storing data

Recording and keeping qualitative data
Recording and keeping quantitative data
What is a spreadsheet and what is a database?
Setting up a spreadsheet/database
Confidentiality and protecting your
database/spreadsheet

OVERVIEW

As we gather data we need to find a useful and safe way of storing them. It is not very practical for analysis to keep piles of questionnaires in a box or a tower of tapes, as the data are not accessible in this form and it will be difficult to find the data we need. As we gather the data we need to put them into a computer database or transcribe them so that we can see more easily what data we have. However, as we start to record the data and put them in a form that we can access, we might be changing these. For example, we might be attaching codes to specific answers. Therefore, we need to make sure we are storing our raw and coded data in the best ways possible for analysing these in the future.

Recording and keeping qualitative data

The operation of listening to a tape and writing down what is recorded on the tape is called transcribing, as explained in Chapter 6. The best way to transcribe tapes is to go straight onto a computer. It is important to decide on the level of detail we want to include in the transcription and to be consistent throughout. For example, we might want to include expressions which indicate emphasis, and there are 'transcription conventions' which we can use to identify these aspects if we want. For example:

(.)	Pause too short to be timed.
(4.0), (2.1)	Pause long enough to be timed in seconds.
If you [began [but you	Square brackets are used to denote overlapping speech and where the overlap begins.

| (...) | Untranscribeable words. |
| I was **not happy** | Italics or bold can be used to signal a speaker's emphasis. |

We also need to decide whether to include long pauses, laughter or sighs which demonstrate how a respondent is feeling. These things can be very useful when it comes to analysing the data, but a straightforward record of the actual words spoken might be adequate for our purpose. The level of detail included in a transcript depends on the type of analysis we will be doing. The most detailed level of analysis of transcripts is called conversation analysis and requires transcripts which are extremely detailed in terms of emphasis, overlaps of speech, and timed length of pauses. It is unlikely that we would use this method in a small-scale evaluation. Careful transcription of the words spoken together with a clear indication of who spoke and when a person interrupts is probably enough for most evaluations (Figure 8.1). Here is an example of how we might transcribe a segment of an interview:

Interviewer HD:	What do you know about your diabetes, following the results of the tests that you have had done?
Patient.	Very little.
HD:	Okay, so you would have had your results from Dr … one of the doctors in the surgery?
Patient.	Yes.
HD:	What did he say to you?
Patient.	Well he said very little, he had the screen in front of him, the video, you know and what he said was 'oh you know it is a little bit sort of iffy', type of thing. You know I can't quote the words he said exactly, 'well' he said 'you know' he said, 'the thing is you have been doing good' he said. 'So we will continue' he said 'to see you as we have done, you know, twice a year' he said and 'keep an eye on everything' and that was virtually about it. He might have said something about putting me to see a Consultant okay, but I am not absolutely certain about that. But that was the end and you know, as far as I knew, I was walking out of there without any undue problems you know. There was nothing sort of put to me, options or about this that or the other, so your phone call to me then was actually out of the blue.

Figure 8.1   Transcription of an interview

| *Interviewer*: | Can you tell me what you felt about the waiting area? |
| *Mr D*: | I found it very depressing, er, there were not enough seats so people were standing around as well as sitting in the small space and there was an awful noise from the piped music, very loud, very distressing if you're feeling anxious. |

Many interviewers include a short summary of how they felt the interview went and any main points they want to note at the end of the interview when they record it (see Figure 8.2).

I found this a difficult and depressing interview: the participant was ill, had been unable to wash themselves and the surroundings were clearly in need of attention. Mr B was constantly interrupted by the dogs and cats which were occupying the room with us and much of the talk on the tape is inaudible or fragmented with the interruptions of the animals. However, Mr B was very emphatic about the need for people to be able to access transport to the clinic and although this may not be very clear on the tape he was keen that taxi telephone numbers or a bus timetable or information telephone numbers should be provided, with a map for access to the clinic. Overall he had not enjoyed his visit to the clinic and would prefer to attend the GP surgery if he did not have to wait too long to be seen there. He did not feel the specialist expertise available at the hospital clinic offered any advantages worth having, as his treatment was the same as that which had been recommended by the GP.

Figure 8.2   Example of an interview summary

These summaries can be very useful in reminding us of some relevant detail, especially if we are transcribing interviews some time after the event. It is best to transcribe these at the end of the interview and add any additional commentary or early coding that seems appropriate at the time when the interview is transcribed. It is possible to buy or borrow a special transcribing machine operated by a foot pedal for transcribing tapes. This is an essential part of equipment for transcribing tapes as we really need both hands free to do a good job of transcription and the foot-operated machine allows us to easily replay sections of tape a number of times and at different speeds if we wish.

It is essential that we ensure data are protected by a password if anyone might have access to the computer other than ourselves. It is best to set up separate files and folders for the evaluation project and ensure that all transcripts are properly labelled in a way which ensures that we can identify which data have come from which source. If we devise a scheme for anonymising the transcripts as we produce them – for example, by changing all the names of individuals – it is essential that we keep a separate file where we can record the original names and the pseudonyms that we have chosen. Copies of field notes and other records of observations should also be stored securely on a computer and of course all documents should be copied onto a disk so that they are safely backed up!

The types of files we might have on a computer are:

Folder: Interview transcripts
        Interview 1 with patient GH
        Interview 2 with patient WE
        Interview 3 with patient YN
        Interview 4 with patient SB
Folder: Codes from analysis of interviews
        Direct quotes from transcripts related to codes
Folder: Anonymisation schedule (may wish to store this and back up in a separate location from the other file)
Folder: Analysis of codes in relation to (1) feelings, (2) knowledge, (3) access, (4) improvements in service

There are a number of computer programs which can be used to analyse qualitative data (such as NUDIST, Ethnograph v5.0, Atlas ti), but they all basically share the ability to sort data into various categories. We should always seek expert advice if we want to use one of these programs, but many of the operations which they perform are feasible in word-processing packages. For example, word-processing packages can be used for coding at the sentence level of transcripts of interviews. We can create a file with a field for the sentence, this field would be called TEXT, and another (or several, perhaps one for each family of coding categories) to hold a set of CODEWORDS, and one that gives each sentence a number, called NUMBERS. This effectively duplicates the process of writing marginal notes when working with paper. Sentences are then coded by typing the names of coding categories in the CODEWORDS field. When this is complete, categories can be extracted by searches and sorts, and printed. You can always return the transcript to its original context by sorting using NUMBERS.

In summary: When recording qualitative data, we need a system to record the coding, quotes and our analysis of codes.

Recording and keeping quantitative data

Quantitative data by their very nature are in the form of spreadsheets or databases.

What is a spreadsheet and what is a database?

A spreadsheet is just a big page where we can record all the data we have gathered. We can record all the types of data we want and sort it in order as well as do statistical tests and calculations. Microsoft Excel is one example of a spreadsheet (see Figure 8.3).

A database can be just like a spreadsheet and can also be one big page to keep data, or it can be a number of pages (spreadsheets) added together and linked. A database is more sophisticated for getting answers from the data (for querying the data), but cannot really be used to do calculations and statistical tests. Data entry can be easier and safer with a database, where it is possible to build in limits and a user-friendly interface. Microsoft Access is one example of a database.

Generally, for a small study, a spreadsheet is the best thing to use as we can fit all the data onto one page and do some of the analysis using this spreadsheet. However, if we are using routine data in which there are thousands of records with vast amounts of information, then we might need to use a database. A database organises the data into different tables. So, for example, we might have the patient's contact details in one table, the patient's first clinical visit in another table, and the patient's medication in another table. All these tables might be linked by the patient's ID number. If we want to look at all the details of one patient, these different tables can be linked up to make a whole new table about just this one patient. Or if we

Patient ID	Sex	Date of birth	Date of diagnosis	Visit date	Age at visit*	Disease duration at visit **	First symptoms: Weight loss Coded data 0 = no, 1 = yes
SB121173	F	12/11/1973	01/01/2001	14/02/2007	33	6.12 years	0
PB140359	M	14/03/1959	12/03/2005	13/03/2005	46	0 years	1
HS131242	F	13/12/1942	14/05/2000	02/03/2005	62	4.8 years	0

Notes:
*formula is (visit date – date of birth)/365))
**formula is (visit date – date of diagnosis)/365))

Figure 8.3   Example of a spreadsheet of results

want to look up the contact details of everyone who attended clinic on one particular day, then we can extract the details of just those patients with a visit on a chosen day. However, to do our analysis we will need to export or move the data we are interested in into a spreadsheet or statistical package.

Setting up a spreadsheet/database

As with everything, before starting it is essential to plan. Often people are tempted just to take a questionnaire and put labels across the top of the spreadsheet, with Q1, Q2, Q3 to represent question 1, question 2 and so on. This allows us to get all the information onto a computer but may not be the best set-up for the analysis we want to do later. It is better to plan what we are going to do with the data and then set up the spreadsheet to facilitate this. For example, think about how many rows and columns we might need, which types of data relate to other types and thus the logical order for recording the data. The purpose of the spreadsheet is to create a place were we can search and analyse the data. We do not want to create a massive grid that is impossible to sort, search and analyse. Here are some essential tips:

1. Get a book on the spreadsheet package that you will be using (for example, a book on MS Excel). This will give the basics for setting up a spreadsheet and is essential if you don't already have experience with spreadsheets.
2. Label the field (the headings at the top) with something that makes sense to the data contained in it. It is not a great idea to label a field with Q1 or with initials that only you can understand, like FL (fatigue level). You might come back two months later to look at the spreadsheet and not remember what the initials meant, or someone else using the spreadsheet will need you to translate before they understand the data.
3. Categorise things so that analysis is easy. For example, we have a list of medication names. Some people put aspirin, some put painkiller, some will misspell, some will write Asprin, and some will put NSAID (non-steroidal anti-inflammatory drug). We will then find it very hard to analyse this as the computer will not be able to work out which two drugs are actually the same thing. It will see Asprin, aspirin, NSAID and pain killer (aspirin) as four separate drugs. What we really want is to categorise drugs according to the way we will analyse the information. If we are going to analyse families of drugs we should just put NSAID for all the drugs in this family. We will want to minimise the number of errors in putting in the data (that is, misspellings) and facilitate the analysis in the end by sorting out some of the data into the categories we want to analyse.
4. Don't put spaces in the spreadsheet to separate data. People sometimes leave a row blank in order to separate different blocks of data, for example, all patients with a surname beginning with A from all those with a surname beginning with B. This is what we might do in a Word document. However, it is not appropriate for a spreadsheet. When we come to sort fields (that is, we ask the computer to put everyone in alphabetic order), the computer will stop where there is a space, so we will not be able to sort our data properly if we have blank rows.

5. Do put spaces in the spreadsheet to separate data from formulae. For example, we may have worked out the average at the bottom of the column of data regarding age. We *do* want a space between the data of participant's ages and the average age. This means we can tell the difference between collected data and the data we have calculated (the average). When we come to sort the data, the computer will therefore not sort the average calculation in with the collected data and we do want them to remain separate.

Be consistent

CHECK THE DATA

CHECK THE INPUT

6. Be consistent. In everything we do we need to make sure we enter the data in the same consistent way throughout the spreadsheet. If we enter a data item as 11/12/06 in one place, we do not want to enter other dates as 12 Dec 2006. If we have data entered in different ways this will affect what we can do with them. For example, if we wanted to work out a person's age at diagnosis we can have their date of diagnosis as 14/1/2004 and the computer can take this away from their date of birth – if it was written as 12/11/1973, but not if it was written as 12 Nov 1973. This is especially important if more than one person is entering data. We need to have an agreement as to how data will be entered so that they are consistent. For example, would the name O'Conner be entered as O'Conner or O'Conner or even Conner? For people with double surnames, such as Cabrera-Rode, would we enter this with Rode as the surname and Cabrera as a middle name, or Cabrera-Rode or Cabrera Rode as the surname? This is all-important in how the database will sort names. If we are not consistent, then people called O'Conner will be put at different places in the spreadsheet (some will be at the top of the Os, as O comes before Oa, some will be in the middle of the Os, as OC will be after Ob and before Od, and some will be with the Cs as Connor would be with these names).

7. Enter some of the data yourself. Often we pay someone else to enter the data. However, if we don't do some of it ourselves, then we won't be able to identify where the errors and problems might be. For example, if we enter some of the data ourselves at the beginning, we will get a feel for which questions are often missed by participants, which we are likely to make a mistake on when entering the data (for example, drug dosage), which the participants are likely to make mistakes on (for example, spelling of drug name), which questions the data entry clerk needs to make subjective decisions on, and how this can be made more objective.

8. Put limits on allowable data so that data entry mistakes are fewer. For example, do not allow a patient age of more than 120 to be inputted.

9. Check the data. Someone independent of the data entry person needs to double-check some of the data entered. For example, every tenth questionnaire should be double-checked by an independent person to check for accuracy in entering the data.

10. Make back-ups and save the data regularly. Also save frequently to avoid losing work, as computers do freeze and crash and lose unsaved

information. Do make copies of the database. If we make a mistake and delete a column by accident or we sort data without highlighting all the fields (so data sort in a random, unlinked way and are then unusable), we need to have a back-up copy of the original database. It is useful, once all the data have been entered and checked and the data collection is completed, to save a copy of this final database. Then we should do the analysis and all the sorting and manipulating of the data on a separate copy. We must never change or manipulate the final database. This means that if we make a mistake we can always go back to the unaltered original and make another copy to analyse.

Confidentiality and protecting your database/spreadsheet

Once data are put onto a computer, then potentially they are at risk of someone hacking into or just logging onto the computer and taking lots of personal and private data which are confidential. When people give their information, then we are required by law (the Data Protection Act in the UK) to treat it as confidential and to protect it from being misused. We should keep all identifiable data separate from clinical data. For example, name, date of birth, hospital number and home address should all be kept in one spreadsheet (with a patient ID number related to the study). This spreadsheet should be protected by a password so that only named people can have access to this identifiable data. The computer should not be connected to the Internet, or should be protected by a firewall and other methods of preventing access to the data from outside. The clinical data should be held separately from the identifiable data. These two spreadsheets should only be linked by the patient ID number within the study/evaluation, so that people outside the study should not be able to identify any of the participants if they access the clinical data. If we need to send information to others, we should not e-mail any identifiable data. Clinical data which do not have any personal identifiers may be e-mailed (ideally with the attached file having password protection). The best way to give these to someone else who is allowed access would be to put the data onto a CD, password protect, these and post them.

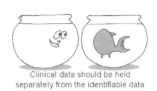

Clinical data should be held separately from the identifiable data

The Data Protection Act relates to paper documents as well as to computer records, so questionnaires should be kept in a locked and secure area where unauthorised people cannot access the data.

Summary

- Think about the level of analysis we need to do, for example, for qualitative interview data, we need to transcribe expressions, emphases and pauses in conversational analysis, as these details are not recorded in a simpler form of transcription and analysis.
- Record short summaries of how the interview went and points we would like to remember later about the interview.

- Password protect all data held on a computer.
- A spreadsheet is one page of data on which we can do statistical analysis.
- A database is a number of pages of data that can be linked together and data can be extracted in different ways, but generally we cannot do statistical analysis with this program.
- We should enter some data ourselves to practise the type of calculations we want to do with the data and to make sure early on that we are recording things in the best way.
- Keep a separate hard copy of the final database. Only work on and do tests on copies of the database. Do not work on the only copy of the database, because if we make a mistake we will have to enter the data again.

Frequently asked questions

I plan to carry out my analysis direct from tapes of interviews – how should I best store these data?

Although it is possible to do the analysis direct from the tapes by taking notes rather than a full transcription of what was said, there are some dangers in this. It is difficult to be really systematic and thorough if a full transcript is not available to check against and from which you can select quotes. You should keep tapes locked away as they contain confidential information, and the transcripts should also be kept in a locked area; the electronic version of the transcripts should also be password protected on the computer.

Once I have transcribed and coded my data and made arrangements to keep these files safely on my computer, can I destroy the original tapes?

No, the tapes are the raw data and the evidence of what was said at the interviews. If you publish your results and someone wants to know more about what was said, or wishes to question your findings, the tapes can be used to support your research.

How long should I keep my data?

We should keep data for at least five years so that other people can double-check your findings at a later date. If anyone is going to question the data, they should do so within five years of the study being published. Your local Research Ethics Committee or Research Governance Committee may specify requirements in addition to this, which you should check.

I am in a hurry, nearing a deadline and do not have enough time to label all my variables in my Excel database – is it OK to input the data and carry out my analysis and put in labels later?

No, because you are unlikely to know what they mean later. You will analyse the wrong data and make errors. You should not be carrying out the analysis in a hurry as this is the ideal way to come up with the wrong answers. Data should be checked for errors before any analysis – if you are in such a hurry you might miss this step and so come up with complete rubbish because you did not do it properly. Try to renegotiate your deadline and avoid cutting corners!

I have started my analysis and found one or two inputting errors – should I correct them? Do I need to do anything else?

Yes, correct all errors. Before doing any analysis you should 'clean' your data. This means look at the maximum and minimum data in each field (column), and for any inconsistencies between fields, for example, implausible combinations such as sex = male *and* pregnancy = yes. So if, say, we have a maximum age of 112 and a minimum age of 0, we need to double-check the inputting of the data and correct these fields. We need to keep doing this until all the data appear to be accurate. We can go to the original data (perhaps the questionnaire) and randomly check some of the entries in the computer with the questionnaire. It is very important that before doing any analysis we have 'cleaned' the data and made sure all of these are believable and accurate.

If I find some obvious errors in respondents' answers on the questionnaire, should I correct them before inputting?

There is a very fine line in correcting errors and putting words into the mouths of respondents. We need to report the findings as they are accurately, even if we think a respondent is wrong. For example, a respondent says they had an injury on a road in one part of the questionnaire and then in another part they say it happened at home. We don't know which is the right answer (possibly they had an injury on their driveway). We cannot complete this correctly but have to accept both answers as right. However, if a respondent says they were born in 12/11/2006 (the day they completed the questionnaire), it is obvious they made a mistake and answered the question wrongly. If we know we can go and look up their medical notes and get their true date of birth, then it seems acceptable that we would complete this part of the questionnaire correctly. However, it is a fine line and a personal judgement as to how much we can 'correct' respondents' answers and thus answer for them.

Further reading

D. Gookin (2003) *Word for Dummies*. Chichester: Wiley.

G. Harvey (2006) *Excel for Dummies*. Chichester: Wiley.

Udo Kelle (2007) Computer-assisted qualitative data analysis, in C. Seale, G. Gobo, J.F. Gubrium and D. Silverman (eds), *Qualitative Research Practice*. London: Sage.

Eben Weitzman and Matthew B. Miles (1995) *Computer Programs for Qualitative Data Analysis: A software sourcebook:* Thousand Oaks, CA: Sage.

Web pages
www.soc.surrey.ac.uk/sru/SRU1.html
www.excel-vba.com/index-excel.htm

9 Analysing Data

We have now reached the best bit of the evaluation, the point where we find out the answers. This is the part where all the planning and designing pays off. We should start out on this phase of the work with a very clear and agreed idea of what analysis we will carry out, from our plan, in order to answer our evaluation questions.

The first step in analysing data is to describe the sample

We first need to say a bit about our sample or about the people who participated in our evaluation. How many men and women (male to female ratio), their average age (maximum and minimum ages) and any other factors that might be relevant, for example, in a diabetes population we might report average disease duration (time from diagnosis), the proportion of smokers and so on. This puts our sample in context so others can see how generalisable our sample will be to their area. For example, if I interview ten male GPs in my local area whose average age is 58 (minimum age 51 and maximum age 64), can we be sure that this will give a good representation of GPs' views in general?

How to analyse qualitative data

There are different ways of approaching the data we have collected, and to some extent these will depend on what resources are available to us in terms of expertise and time. One of the most important operations which we need to carry out on the data is sorting and coding, and an important aspect of these can be counting, to get a broad sense of whether most, very few or none of our respondents are saying something. We also need to get a sense of how strongly people are expressing their opinions. These two basic quantitative operations are always essential when we begin analysing qualitative data, and as soon as we begin to describe results in terms like more, fewer, less, very strongly, we should be aware that we need to have ensured that those descriptions are actually clearly linked to our data.

There are a number of computer programs which can be used to analyse qualitative data but they all basically share the ability to sort data into various categories. We should always seek expert advice if we want to use one of these programs, but many of the operations which they perform are feasible in word-processing packages. For example, it is always possible to make a new file to store every example of a particular type of response to one question. So you might want to start new files for all the examples in your data which referred to a new treatment option in positive terms. This would allow you to readily store quotes and examples which you might use in the final report.

Structured interviews

If we have asked people the same questions in the same order – whether face to face or on the telephone –we will then be faced with a number of answers to the same question. Our first task is to make sure we have all the answers in a readable format, stored on a computer for easy management.

Transcribe the interviews: The first step is to transcribe all the interviews so that we can see what each respondent has said and that it is available to us in a form which allows us to organise our data. We need to sort these answers into an order which can allow us to identify readily whether most people are saying the same thing or whether there is wide variation in the answers to each particular question. In some ways the responses are already sorted for us as all the answers to a particular question will be easily identifiable.

Code the interviews: Our next step is to reduce the large quantity of data available to us into a form where we can be reasonably sure that we are accurately representing the range of different responses or the strength of commitment to one answer if everyone has said roughly the same thing. In order to work this out our first task is coding the text. This involves labelling all text which refers to the same issue in the same way so that we can easily identify all the text which refers to one issue. This will help us to make sure that we answer the evaluation questions as thoroughly as possible.

```
Waiting room experience

[Code]                          [Text]
01                              Depressing colour on walls
02                              Annoying music
03                              Waited too long with no information
04                              Skylight full of bird droppings
05                              Reception staff pleasant/agreeable/helpful
06                              Comfortable environment (seating/reading material)
07                              Difficult to hear name being called (due to 02)
08                              Crowded
09                              Music relaxing/enjoyable
```

Figure 9.1   Coding

For example, if we have asked patients how they feel about the waiting room at the rapid access chest pain clinic, we need to be sure that we include in our report the finding that three-quarters of our respondents complained about the loud, piped music being played, but that some people did not notice this and that a small minority enjoyed the music. We will only be able to do this if we have found a way to bring together all the information we have about piped music in the interviews and coding allows us to do this. See Figure 9.1 for an example of how things might be coded.

In carrying out our analysis we are reducing the large number of different responses into a form which represents what people told us and includes all the information we judge to be important. One of the most difficult aspects of analysing qualitative data is that you have to be willing to take responsibility for deciding on what to leave out of any final report. In a straightforward investigation of people's views this should not be too difficult, although all projects will present us with some dilemmas about what to include and how much. The guiding framework for all analysis should be the aims and the objectives of the study – remember the questions you are trying to answer and try to ensure that your report is answering the question. But make a note of any other themes coming out of the data, as they might indicate that the research did not capture everything that was important to respondents.

Semi-structured interviews

Analysing the findings from semi-structured interviews can be very time consuming, but it is important to be systematic in the analysis if the results are to justify the time we have put into the data collection and analysis. The best way to record interviews is to audio tape them; it is very difficult to take notes that adequately record all that people said in the interview and to be able to be listening to every word at the same time. The most thorough approach is to transcribe all the interviews so that we are able to manage a set of 'transcripts' on a computer. If we do the transcription ourselves, this can be a very valuable way of reminding us of what people said. If we have arranged for someone else to do it, we need to check the transcripts against the tapes, correcting any differences as we go along.

Once we have all the transcripts or records constructed from notes, the next stage is to code the transcripts. This means that we should go through each interview in detail, identifying themes and issues and labelling them so that we can easily find them again and bring together all the similar bits of interviews. Alternatively, we might need to identify themes that people had strong views about but disagreed on, such as the piped music at the clinic.

Development of themes: Once you have been through all the transcripts coding them, it is important to share our work with other team members (if this is possible); if more than one team member is coding transcripts, it is essential that they compare their work and ensure that the same types of theme or issue are being labelled with the same code. Researchers need to reach a shared understanding that they can agree on at the end of the study, as differences over coding can create problems for later interpretation and presentation. So, for example, if we have coded all our responses to the questions about what patients felt about a clinic, we will have a number of different types of responses, perhaps coded under positive and negative responses in the first instance and then with codes under two broad headings such as: negative length of wait; discomfort during wait; a lack of seating; a lack of toilet facilities; distance from car park; difficulties in public transport; a lack of clear directions; a lack of information provided about what would happen; doctor didn't explain why treatment was given; not enough privacy in changing rooms; noise from barking dogs; noisy piped music.

When all the transcripts have been coded and agreement has been reached that coding is consistent across those who have done the coding, the next step is to organise the findings into a coherent report. This is often experienced as being very difficult by the novice, but once again our aims and objectives can guide us – we need to identify the answers which bear on these and only these, so we can decide which segments of our data are relevant to which questions or objectives by going through the coded transcripts and our objectives describing what we have found under each heading. Once again, we are reducing data to a manageable form in order to respond to our original questions.

So following through the example above, we now need to identify which of our patient responses are relevant to the questions regarding the clinic. We need to identify the responses we have coded under themes. These themes can then be reported more generally. We must sort through the codes and decide which fit together under a theme – for example, in the list above, distance from car park, lack of clear directions and difficulties with public transport will all fit together within a theme which can be called 'physical access to the clinic'. This theme can be paired with the positive findings we have coded in relation to physical access. Thus we will have a section in our report which describes physical access to the clinic for patients and we might as a result want to recommend relocation, closer timing of the clinic with bus timetables and so on.

> *Motivators and facilitators to insulin therapy*
>
> One person who had commenced insulin therapy prior to the interview suggested that she had a 'positive' experience in 'adapting' to an insulin regime, had 'no problems with injecting insulin' and had 'more flexibility with her diet' since taking insulin. She also felt she had 'more energy'. Another person who also progressed to insulin therapy explained 'it's a small price to pay for health' and it had made him 'feel healthy and reasonably well'. Other people (4/10) acknowledged that insulin does help in preserving the body's own natural insulin supply, and one person decided to go on insulin rather than taking OHA to manage their diabetes on this premise. One person suggested that if insulin came in a tablet format, then he would choose to go on insulin sooner rather than later in the disease process. The information booklet was viewed as providing food for thought on insulin treatment and management decisions for people with diabetes. However, 'time' was needed to adjust to the diagnosis of diabetes and the possibility and often inevitability of using insulin for glycaemia control.

Figure 9.2   Report from qualitative data

Findings need to be presented logically and as representatively as possible. The best way to get an idea of how to write a report using qualitative data is to look at some examples, and there are also some useful texts which offer advice on this (references at the end of this chapter) and Figure 9.2 also provides an example.

Focus groups

Focus groups can be the most difficult data source to reduce to manageable formats. The main reason for this is that it can be difficult to work out who is saying what. For some groups it is important to be able to identify who said what. For example, if we have men and women in one focus group, we will want to know if men give different answers from women to some questions. Or we might have a mix of ages and it might be that younger people feel differently about an issue than older people. So the careful transcription or recording of focus groups is an important first step.

Coding is the next step in analysing these transcripts, just as it was for interviews, and once again the process is to facilitate our production of a sensible reduction of a large amount of information into a report which allows us to answer the research questions. Some people find it helpful to have separate computer files or even large pieces of paper for each objective of the evaluation and to bring together in that file or on that piece of paper all the items coded with labels which are or can be related to the question. Again this is a process which is most helpful if carried out as a team activity. It is certainly very helpful to share the way in which the connections are being made between the question and the codes as information is sorted in this way, and a team meeting just for this purpose can be very useful. Remember that:

- Coding should be done by two or more individuals.
- Coding should be checked and validated.
- Codes should be sorted into themes which relate to the aims and objectives of the evaluation.
- Relationships between codes and themes need to be discussed by two or more individuals whenever possible.

Understanding observation data

This depends on the format in which the information has been recorded. If a structured observation schedule has been devised which allows people to count, for example, the number or frequency of an event, then analysis will depend on carrying out some simple operations on counting totals, such as number of interruptions during a consultation or looking at contextualising features like time of day or number of staff on duty.

If a less structured approach has been used, then it is likely that you will have a body of data which consists of texts in the form of field notes. These can be coded and analysed in the same way as the texts of interview transcripts – carefully relating the codes to the evaluation aims and objectives. So, for example, if you have observed the waiting room at the rapid access clinic you might have field notes something like that shown in Figure 9.3.

In summary:

- We can use a computer program to help with coding transcripts.
- Once manuscripts have been coded we need to look at themes and work with others to develop the broad ideas and themes that will emerge from the data.
- Analysis should be informed by and aimed at answering the aims and objectives of the study.

How to analyse quantitative data

Please read Chapter 7 before attempting this section.

The most important question

The planning stage of the evaluation

When planning the evaluation we should have developed a clear idea of what is the most important question. This is the primary outcome variable. In other words, what is the single most important thing that we want to show or evaluate in our study? This is the question that we used to do our sample size (power) calculation and decide the number of people or sample size we needed. Our evaluation should have the power or the ability to answer at least a single question. So before we even started collecting data we should know what question we want to answer and how we might do this. For example, what if we want to know if the introduction of a new midwife-led birthing unit in a hospital has improved births for women in that hospital. To do this we need to think about what we mean by 'improved births' and to think about these being improved relative to what? We might choose to say improved is defined as 'fewer medical interventions', for example, induced labours, the use of aids such as forceps, or emergency caesareans. We might say fewer medical interventions – relative to the way the hospital was before the unit was

I arrive at 9.15, lights on in waiting room, door to outside locked but bearing a notice that says DOORS WILL BE OPENED at 9 a.m.

9.30 Nurse arrives but 17 patients waiting outside locked door in the rain: Nurse makes cup of tea while sorting through files, takes cup of tea through to doctor's room. 9.37 Nurse then unlocks door and patients enter, some sit down but some remain standing. Nurse leaves and goes into doctor's room without any interaction with patients, two patients complain loudly about long wait and that appointment time has already passed. Nurse returns to desk and sits, and male, elderly, patient (1) approaches, clearly in discomfort. Nurse stands up, with file in her hand, moves back towards doctor's room, reaching for switch on the wall which turns on loud piped music. She then turns to p1 and tells him to take a seat. P1 clearly doesn't hear and asks where the toilets are but nurse has already re-entered dr's office. P1 looks around presumably for signs to toilets but there appear to be none. 9.50 Dr (male, mid 40's) arrives and walks straight into office and closes door.

We could code the description above in the following way:

I arrive at 9.15, lights on in waiting room, door to outside locked but bearing a notice that says DOORS WILL BE OPENED at 9 a.m. (LACK OF INFORMATION, POOR COMMUNICATION)

9.30 Nurse arrives but 17 patients waiting outside locked door in the rain. (TIMING, POOR FACILITIES FOR WAITING)

Nurse makes cup of tea while sorting through files, takes cup of tea through to doctor's room. (LACK OF CONSIDERATION FOR PATIENTS) 9.37 Nurse then unlocks door and patients enter, some sit down but some remain standing. (COMFORT IN WAITING ROOM) Nurse leaves and goes into doctor's room without any interaction with patients, (LACK OF INFORMATION, POOR COMMUNICATION) two patients complain loudly about long wait and that appointment time has already passed. Nurse returns to desk and sits, and male, elderly, patient (1) approaches, clearly in discomfort. Nurse stands up, with file in her hand, moves back towards doctor's room, reaching for switch on the wall which turns on loud piped music. (MUSIC) She then turns to p1 and tells him to take a seat. P1 clearly doesn't hear and asks where the toilets are but nurse has already re-entered dr's office. P1 looks around presumably for signs to toilets but there appear to be none. (LACK OF INFORMATION) 9.50 Dr (male, mid 40's) arrives and walks straight into office and closes door. (TIMING)

The relevant codes are in brackets after the segment that they refer to and you could choose to edit the description further by highlighting all the references to TIMING, for example, and placing them in one file, or you could choose to work with all the negative codes in one file and positives in another.

Figure 9.3   Transcription of observation data

introduced *and* relative to a control hospital that did not have a midwife-led unit added to the hospital. Why do we need this control hospital? (Answer in Chapter 10, under Observation without a control group.)

We know that we are going to be comparing numbers of women having a medical intervention before and after the unit and in a different hospital, so we can now make sure we understand how to analyse these data, and to make sure we collect these data accurately. Before starting it is important to talk to a statistician about our plans. Just talking things through with someone else is important – even statisticians get advice from each other. So no matter what our previous knowledge or ability, always talk the plan through with others who have experience in statistics or the analysis of quantitative data.

The basics

When we are analysing quantitative data we are taking a sample of participants and examining if one group is different from another group. In the analysis we want to establish:

Is there a difference in our sample?

- If there is a difference in our sample?
- How likely it is that this difference in the sample exists in the population.
- How likely it is that we have made a mistake (that the difference in the sample occurred by chance)

  or

that our sample did not find a difference but a real difference exists in the population.

The types of statistical tests we use depend on the type of data we have. If we have ratio data and if the *population* that our sample comes from is normally distributed, we can use *parametric tests*. These include T-tests and Pearson's correlation. These are the tests used on data that are normally distributed.

If we have ordinal or nominal data or we know that the population we are taking a sample from is not normally distributed, then we use *non-parametric tests*. These include Chi-squared and Spearman's rank order correlation tests (see Figure 9.4).

In parametric tests (that is, those with ratio data such as age, weight, and height from a normal distribution) the figures we will need to understand are:

- The mean is the average for normally distributed data.
- The standard deviation is used to describe how well the mean reflects all the data in the sample, for example, 95 per cent of the sample will be within two standard deviations of the mean.
- The standard error tells us where the population average might be. It is a number which tells us about the sampling error. That is the error we get from just taking a sample, and not the whole population.
- The 95 per cent confidence interval tells us about the difference between two things in the population. We will be 95 per cent confident that the amount of difference between two things is within this range (given by the 95 per cent confidence interval, see Chapter 7).

Before we start our parametric test we need to think about what type of questions we want to answer:

- If we want to compare the average (mean) in two different groups – for example, the average age of women treated in our hospital compared to the control hospital – we will use a T-test.
- If we want to look at the relationship between two types of continuous data – for example, the weight of the mother compared to the weight of the baby across the range – we will use correlation.
- If we want to compare proportions of something in two different groups – for example, the number of women who have labour induced in the

Parametric tests

Comparing:	Example:	Test:
Two means	Age of the men in a sample compared to the women	T-test
	Ratio data (age) compared in two nominal groups (men/women)	
Relationship between two types of ratio data	The weight of the baby compared to the weight of the mother	Pearson's correlation
	Ratio data (weight of mother) compared to ratio data (weight of baby)	
Two means in one sample	Pain level before taking a drug and pain level after taking a drug	Matched/paired T-test

Non-parametric tests

Two proportions	Number of smokers among the women compared to the men in the sample	Chi-squared test
Relationship between two types of ordinal data	Injury severity score as assessed by doctor A and as assessed by doctor B	Spearman's rank order correlation

Figure 9.4 Ways of analysing numbers (statistical tests on quantitative data)

hospital before the midwife unit and after the midwife-led unit – we will use Chi-squared.

*   If we want to look at the relationship between two types of discrete data – for example, the level of tear and the use of medical interventions – we will use Spearman's rank correlation.

In the next section we are going to work through some examples using statistics pages found on the Internet. However, if you work with a statistician they will use a statistics program like SPSS or STATA. Many of these statistics tests (Chi-squared and Pearson's correlation) can be done on Excel. If we use the help menus on Excel, they will tell us how to do the tests. So there are plenty of resources that we can use to perform the tests, but the important thing is to understand what we are doing and how we interpret the answers.

Parametric tests

T-test

When to use this test: We use this test when we have *two* samples (like men and women). These two samples should have data for which we can calculate a mean and standard deviation (ratio data) such as age, height, length, weight, disease duration, age at onset of disease. We should use this test when we want to see if the average of one sample is different from the average of another sample. So, for example, if we want to examine the impact of a new midwife-led unit in the hospital, first of all we will want to see if the women who went to the unit were the same age as those in the control hospital. To examine this question we would compare the mean ages and use a T-test to look at whether any difference is likely to reflect a real difference in the population, or whether it may be due to chance.

What this test examines: We are using the samples to see what the difference in them tells us about the difference that may exist in the population. This is why we should always report 95 per cent confidence intervals. Confidence intervals tell us what the difference might be in the population based on the mean and the variation seen in the samples. So, for example, we may find out that the average age of our sample of women using the midwife-led birthing unit was 32 and the average age of the women in the control hospital was 28. Does this difference reflect a real difference between the groups?

How to do the test: To do the T-Test go to http://home.clara.net/sisa/ t-test.htm. We need to know:

*   The mean in our samples.
*   The numbers in our samples.
*   The standard deviation in our sample.

Imagine we have a sample of 500 women who used the birthing clinic and 500 women from the control hospital. The average age of the women in the birthing clinic was 32 (standard deviation five years), the average age of the women in the control hospital was 28 (standard deviation seven years). Was there a significant difference?

To do this on the above website:

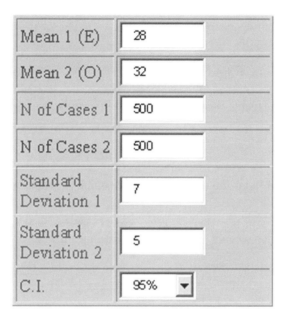

- The first box is the mean age of the women in the control hospital.
- The second box is the mean age of the women in the midwife-led birthing unit.
- The third box is the number in our sample of women in the control hospital.
- The fourth box is the number in our sample of women in the midwife-led unit.
- The fifth box is the standard deviation of the women in the control hospital.
- The sixth box is the standard deviation of the women in the midwife-led unit.
- The C.I. is the confidence interval. This tells us the range of figure where we are 95 per cent confident that the population means/averages may lie.

The answers we will get are:

Mean1 eq: 28 (variance=49) (se=0.3134)
Mean2 eq: 32 (variance=25) (se=0.2238)

Single-sided probability that the two variances are equal (ftest): 0

Difference between means:
−4 (sd=11.5605) (se=0.3847)
95 per cent CI: −4.754<diff<−3.246 (Wald)

T-value of difference: −10.398; df-t: 903
Probability: 0 (left tail pr: 1)
Double-sided p-value: 0
*******ready

Mean1 tells us the average age of the women in the control hospital is 28 (standard error=0.31)
Mean2 tells us the average age of the women in the birthing unit is 32 (standard error=0.223)
The difference between the two means is −4 (standard deviation=11.56) (standard error=0.38)
The 95 per cent confidence interval is between −4.75 to −3.246
The p value is p <0.0001

Interpreting the result:

The average age in our sample is 28. We can be 95 per cent confident* that the population mean of women in the control hospital is: 28 + 2(s.e) or 28 + 2x(0.31) = 28.6

$$28 - 2(s.e) \text{ or } 28 - 2x(0.31) = 27.4$$

The average age of the women in the control hospital (population) is between 27.4 and 28.6.

The average age of in our sample is 32. We are 95 per cent confident that the population mean of women attending the birthing unit is: 32 + 2(s.e) or 32 + 2(0.22) = 32.44

$$32 - 2(s.e) \text{ or } 32 - 2(0.22) = 31.56$$

The average age of the women attending the birthing unit (population) is between 31.5 and 32.4.

The difference in our two samples is 4 years (standard deviation 11.56 years).

We are 95 per cent sure that in the population the difference in average age between women attending the birthing unit and women in the control hospital is between 3.2 years to 4.75 years. Therefore, women in the mid-wife led birthing unit are significantly older than women in the control hospital (p < 0.05).

This p value (<0.0001) tells us that there is a less than 1 in 10,000 chance that we are wrong and women in the birthing unit are not older than women in the control hospital.

Therefore, in summary, we have found out that women attending the birthing unit were older that women in the control hospital. This test can be used to see if any two samples (with ratio data) are different.

Do *not* use this test if:

- The data are not ratio data or do not come from a population which has a normal distribution.
- The two samples are not independent, for example, the same people before a treatment and after a treatment.

_____

*95 per cent confidence intervals are really worked out as 1.97(s.e.). I have used 2 here (rounded up) just to make it simpler, but the true figure should be 1.97.

Correlation

When to use this test: We use this test when we think there is a relation-ship between two types of continuous data. For example, take the response time of an ambulance with distance from the hospital, and the weight of a baby compared to the weight of the mother. Before doing the test we should always plot the data in a scatter diagram. This is simply plotting one vari-able (for example, weight of baby) against the other variable (for example, weight of the mother). We can do this in Excel.

   If we put in the first column all the data on weight of the mother and in the second column all the data on weight of the baby we would get:

[Weight mother (kg)]	[Weight baby (kg)]
54	3.6
57	3.9
64	4.1
90	4.5
105	5.5
51	2.3
57	2.7
57	3.2
64	3.6
64	3.6
70	3.9
45	2.7
45	2.7
115	4.5
102	4.5
89	4.3
89	3.9
64	3.6
64	4.1
57	3.6

If we highlight these cells and click on INSERT in the toolbar at the top and choose CHART (or click on the chart icon):

- We can pick XY (SCATTER) from the menu and then click on NEXT.
- We need to make sure the data series has Columns selected, and then press NEXT.
- We can label our scattergram with a title and label the axis.
- We then can select where to put the scattergram (on a new page of its own or within the sheet with the list of data).
- Then we can choose FINISH and see the scattergram (Figure 9.5).

We can see from this scattergram that there does appear to be a relation-ship between mother weight and baby weight, because as one goes up the other goes up too. We can put a number on how well these two are asso-ciated with each other (how much one goes up with the other) by doing a correlation test.

What this test examines: Correlation tests will give a number called the correlation coefficient. This number tells how much one set of data changes with another set of data. The number is always between 1 (perfect correlation where one goes up with the other) and -1 (perfect correlation where one goes down as the other goes up). If the number is 0, then there is no relationship between the two sets of data (see Figure 9.6).

How to do the test: To do the correlation test go to http://faculty. vassar.edu/lowry/corr_stats.html. Type in the number of measures. For the data above related to mother's weight and baby weight, the number of observations is 20. Type 20 in the SCRIPT PROMPT. Scroll down to DATA ENTRY and type the numbers from above in the cells:

Pairs	Data Cells		Residuals
	X	Y	
1	54	3.6	----
2	57	3.9	----
3	64	4.1	----
4	90	4.5	----
5	105	5.5	----
6	51	2.3	----
7	57	2.7	----
8	57	3.2	----
9	64	3.6	----
10	64	3.6	----
11	70	3.9	----
12	45	2.7	----
13	45	2.7	----
14	115	4.5	----
15	102	4.5	----
16	89	4.3	----
17	89	3.9	----
18	64	3.6	----
19	64	4.1	----
20	57	3.6	----

Click on Calculate.

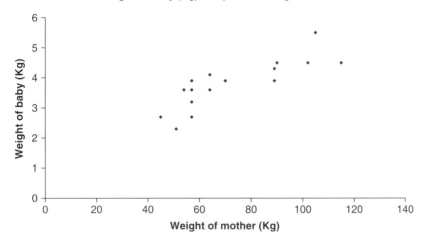

Figure 9.5   Scattergram

The answer we would get should look like this:

Data Summary

$$\Sigma X = \boxed{1403} \qquad \Sigma X^2 = \boxed{106539}$$

$$\Sigma Y = \boxed{74.8} \qquad \Sigma Y^2 = \boxed{290.94}$$

$$\Sigma XY = \boxed{5496.3}$$

	X	Y
N	20	
Mean	70.15	3.74
Variance	427.2921	0.5888
Std.Dev.	20.671	0.7674
Std.Err.	4.6222	0.1716

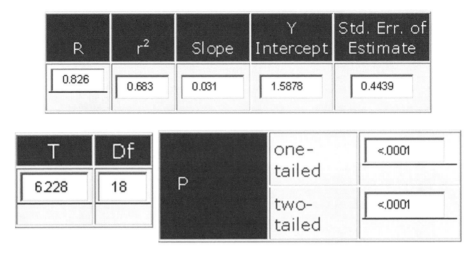

0.95 and 0.99 Confidence Intervals of rho

This tells us that the mean of the mothers' weights was 70.15 kg, the standard deviation was 20.67 kg and the standard error was 4.6. (so we are 95 per cent sure that the mean weight in the population is 70.15 + 2(4.6) and 70.15 – 2(4.6) = 60.95 kg to 79.35 kg).

The mean of the babies' weights was 3.74 kg with a standard deviation of 0.76 kg and a standard error of 0.17 kg. (So we are 95 per cent sure that the mean baby weight in the population is 3.74 + 2(0.17) = 4.08 and 3.74 – 2(0.17) = 3.4. This means the average baby weight in the population is going to be between 3.4 kg and 4.08 kg.)

The correlation coefficient is called *rho* and is represented here by *r*. It measures the strength of the association between the weight of the mother and the weight of a baby. In this case the *r* is 0.826. If 1 is a perfect correlation, then this 0.8 value indicates a strong relationship – as the weight of the mother goes up, so does the weight of the baby.

The r^2 is 0.68, and this tells us that 68 per cent of the babies' weights can be predicted from knowing a mother's weight.

The slope of 0.031 tells us that if we put a line through the points on the scattergraph in Figure 9.5, the slope of that line would be 0.031. Or to put it another way for every kg the mother goes up in weight, the baby weight goes up 0.031 kg.

The Y intercept tells us that if we drew this line through the points on the scattergraph, it would cross the Y axis (the one going up, the vertical axis) at 1.58.

The p value tells us that there is a significant correlation between mothers' weight and babies' weight of $p < 0.0001$. This means the chance that in the population there is not a relationship between mother's weight and baby weight is less than 1 in 10,000.

If 1 is a perfect correlation (see Figure 9.6), we would estimate that in the population the correlation between mother and baby weight could be between 0.6 to 0.9 (we are therefore 95 per cent confident).

Interpreting the result: This means we are confident that there is a relationship between mother's weight and baby's weight. As the mother's weight goes up 1 kg, the baby's weight goes up 0.03 kg. However, knowing there is a relationship does not mean that one causes the other. We cannot say that mothers who are heavy *cause* their baby to be big. We can say that the heavier the mother then the heavier the baby tends to be. But we have not examined the reason. This is an

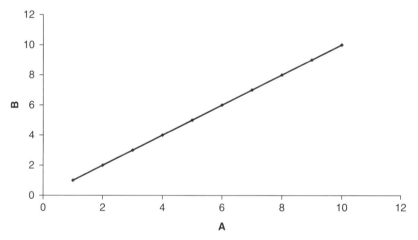

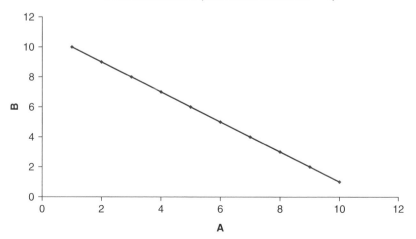

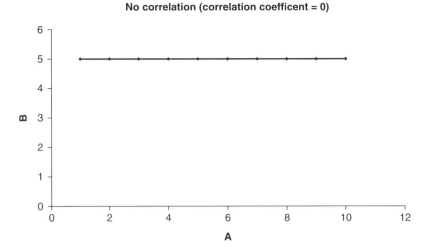

Figure 9.6   Correlation graphs

association and not a proof of cause. Sometimes two variables can appear to be related but the cause can be a separate factor that is related to both, for example, the father's earnings and the length of time the baby is breast-fed. The father is not paying to breast-feed the baby directly and feeding the baby does not generate more money for the father. However, a mother may be more likely to have more time off work (and to breast-feed longer) if she is with a higher earning father.

Non-parametric tests

Chi-squared test

When to use this test: We use this test when we have two (or more) samples (like women and men). The two samples should have data that are nominal (name), or ordinal (in an order). This means we can create proportions from the data, for example, the number of women who have a spontaneous onset of labour among those attending a hospital with a midwife-led unit compared to those attending a hospital without a midwife-led unit. We can use the Chi-squared test when we want to see if the proportions in one sample differ from the proportions in another sample.

What this test examines: The Chi-squared test compares what we observed (number of women having spontaneous labour) with what we expected (if midwife-led units did not have an influence on onset of labour). Therefore, the test examines if what we observe with our sample is so different from what we could have expected, that is, it very unlikely to have occurred by chance.

How to do the test: To do the Chi-squared test we can use Excel.
   We want to examine if women in the hospital with the midwife-led unit had a spontaneous labour more often than women in the hospital without the midwife-led unit.

We examined 1000 births in the hospital with the midwife-led unit and 550 had a spontaneous labour. We examined 1000 births in the hospital without the midwife-led unit and 450 had a spontaneous labour. Does the hospital with the midwife-led unit have more spontaneous labour births? We put what we observed in Excel like this:

	A	B	C	D
1	Observed			
2		MW Unit	Non MW unit	Total
3	Spontaneous	550	450	1000
4	Induced	450	550	1000
5		1000	1000	2000

Then we need to compare this to what we would have expected if there was no difference in spontaneous versus induced births in MW vs Non-MW units. We can probably guess this is 500 in each group if there was no influence of unit, that is there are 2000 people and they should be equally divided in 4 between the 4 possible boxes.

However, if we want to do this 'statistically' and so know how to do it for future calculations the way to get Excel to work out the 'expected' rates is:

	A	B	C	D
1	Observed			
2		MW Unit	Non MW unit	Total
3	Spontaneous	550	450	1000
4	Induced	450	550	1000
5		1000	1000	2000
6				
7	Expected			
8		MW Unit	Non MW unit	Total
9	Spontaneous	=(D3*B5)/D5	=(D3*C5)/D5	1000
10	Induced	=(D4*B5)/D5	=(D4*C5)/D5	1000
11		1000	1000	2000

This will give us 500 in each cell.

We then write the formula for Excel to calculate chi squared. This is CHITEST(observed range, expected range)

So we write in Excel: =chitest(B3:C4,B9:C10). It will give us the p value. In this case the p = 0.0000007. So this is highly significant.

Interpreting the result: The very small p value tells us the chance that we would get this result in our sample, if there was no difference between the MW unit and the non MW unit in the population, is less than 1 in 1,000,000. So our answer in the end is: 55 per cent of women attending the MW unit hospital had a spontaneous birth and 45 percent of women attending the control hospital had a spontaneous birth. Women attending the midwife-led unit hospital are significantly more likely [$p < 0.0000007$] to have a spontaneous birth. However, we cannot prove or say that the midwife-led unit caused women to have more spontaneous births. We can just say that women attending a midwife-led unit are more likely to have a spontaneous birth compared to those attending hospital.

Spearman's rank order correlation

When to use this test: Spearman's rank order correlation is a test to look at the strength of the relationship between two things. Like Pearson's correlation described above, it gives an answer which is between –1 and 1. If a correlation is 1, then there is a perfect straight line between the two sets of data (see Figure 9.6). We use this test when the data we have are ordinal (can be put into order). Generally, if the data are ratio data, we must use Pearson's correlation (described above). However, if we know that the population where the data come from does not have a normal distribution, then we can use Spearman's rank order correlation. Spearman's rank order correlation does not need the data to have a mean and standard deviation, so it can be used on any data that can be given order or ranks.

What this test examines: The test actually orders and ranks all the data in one column and separately ranks and orders all the data in the other column. Then it looks at the difference between the ranks. The value is then a summary of the difference between the ranks, rather than the original data values.

How to do the test: We will need to examine the relationship between number of interventions used and well-being of the baby. The number of interventions can be a total of ten (including methods of induction, pain relief, use of vacuum or forceps, episiotomy etc) and the well-being of the baby is measured on a 1 to 10 scale called the Apgar score. Our data are as follows:

[Number of interventions]	[Apgar Score]
5	4
0	9
2	8
2	7
9	7
3	6

3	7
4	5
8	2
4	2
8	6
0	8
1	8
2	7
8	7
5	7
6	3
2	9
3	10
2	10

Is there a relationship between the number of interventions and the newborn baby's well-being?

- Go to http://faculty.vassar.edu. lowry/corr_**rank**.html
- Type in number 20 at the prompt 'Please enter the number of values of XY pairs'.
- In the 'Raw Data' column (the second set of X Y columns) enter the following:

pairs	Ranks for X	Ranks for Y	Raw Data for X	Raw Data for Y
1			5	4
2			0	9
3			2	8
4			2	7
5			9	7
6			3	6
7			3	7
8			4	5
9			8	2
10			4	2
11			8	6
12			0	8
13			1	8
14			2	7
15			8	7
16			5	7
17			6	3
18			2	9
19			3	10
20			2	10

- Click on 'Calculate from raw data', and the answer you get should look like this:

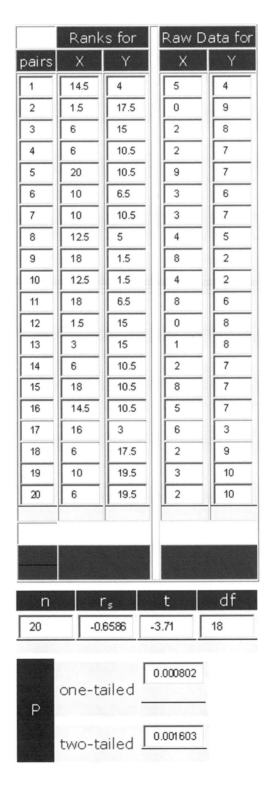

pairs	Ranks for X	Ranks for Y	Raw Data for X	Raw Data for Y
1	14.5	4	5	4
2	1.5	17.5	0	9
3	6	15	2	8
4	6	10.5	2	7
5	20	10.5	9	7
6	10	6.5	3	6
7	10	10.5	3	7
8	12.5	5	4	5
9	18	1.5	8	2
10	12.5	1.5	4	2
11	18	6.5	8	6
12	1.5	15	0	8
13	3	15	1	8
14	6	10.5	2	7
15	18	10.5	8	7
16	14.5	10.5	5	7
17	16	3	6	3
18	6	17.5	2	9
19	10	19.5	3	10
20	6	19.5	2	10

n	r_s	t	df
20	-0.6586	-3.71	18

P

one-tailed   0.000802

two-tailed   0.001603

Interpreting the result: We can see that in the ranks for X and Y columns, the raw values have been given a ranking or order. For example, there were two women who had no interventions so they have both been ranked 1.5 (one should have been ranked #1 and the other #2, but since they have the same value they have been give the average of these two ranks).

The n tells us that there were 20 pairs of data, or 20 measures of babies' well-being and interventions in the labour.

The r_S tells us the slope of the line between these two sets of data. In this case it is −0.66. That is, there is strong negative correlation. As the number of interventions goes up, the babies' well-being scores go down. The number of interventions is associated with poorer well-being for the baby. As we increase the number of interventions, the babies' well-being scores go down by 0.66 on the 0−10 Apgar scale.

Df stands for degrees of freedom and we can ignore this at the moment.

The p value (two-tailed) tells us that the significance is 0.0016 [p = 0.001]. This mean that there is a 1 in 1000 chance that we are wrong and that in the population there is not a relationship between number of interventions and babies' well-being.

However, we cannot say that interventions directly cause babies to be harmed. It is very likely that a woman has more interventions because her baby is in distress. The more distressed the baby, the more likely a woman is to have an emergency caesarean, need pain relief and have surgery. Therefore, we can only say there is a relationship, but we cannot say from our Spearman's findings what causes this relationship.

Other types of tests

There are many other types of tests that can be done. However, we would recommend working with a statistician when doing these tests. These tests are listed below.

Analysis of variance: We can use this when we want to look at the effect of more than one variable on another variable. For example, we may want to know if the number of interventions carried out in labour is associated with age, number of previous pregnancies, size of baby and attendance at the midwife unit or at the control hospital. We could do this with a series of tests, one after another, looking at the relationship between intervention and age, intervention and number of previous pregnancies, intervention and size of baby, intervention and hospital attended and so on. However, this would not be recommended. A p value of a test tell us the probability that we have this finding by chance. So, for example, if we do a test and get a 0.05p value there is a 5 in 100 probability that our findings are by chance (or as a result of sample variation) and are not a 'true' finding. This means that the more tests we do, the higher the likelihood we will accept findings in error. For example, if we do 20 tests in our study (all the factors that could be associated with the number of interventions undertaken), then we would expect by chance alone that one of these would have a p value of p = 0.05. This is a 'significant' p value but this has occurred simply by chance. This means we should try to do as few tests as possible, and set out our analysis plans in advance so that we cannot be accused of 'fishing' and selectively reporting those results that are 'significant' by chance. Please see Case Study 7.2.

The advantage of carrying out a combined test, in which variables are looked at together through analysis of variance, is that we can control for different factors. For example, we can look at the effect of a hospital on number of medical interventions in labour, taking into account (or controlling for) any effects of age of mother, size of baby and so on.

This is a powerful statistics tool that does need a statistician or someone experienced in conducting this type of analysis. How to enter the data into the computer package and what the results mean do require experience and help if you are inexperiened at these. A good explanation can be found at http://en.wikipedia.org/wiki/Analysis_of_variance and at http://bmj.bmj journals.com/cgi/content/full/312/7044/1472

Odds and risk ratios: These can be used when we want to see the probability or chance of one thing happening given another thing has happened. For example, what is the likelihood a woman is induced given she has attended the control hospital instead of the midwife-led unit hospital? The chance is (from the Chi-squared data above):

450/550 (control hospital)
compared to:
550/450 (MW hospital),
so:
550/450 divided by 450/550 = 1.47
She is 1.47 times more likely to be induced in the control hospital than in the MW hospital. This is the odds ratio.

The advantage of this test is that we can work out confidence intervals and so can put the sample result in context with the population (we cannot do this using Chi-squared), but doing it properly and interpreting it properly need advice. We would recommend working with someone with experience for this test. Further information can be found at www. childrens-mercy.org/stats/journal/ oddsratio.asp and http://bmj.bmjjournals.com/epidem/epid.3.html

If you want to do a T-test or a Chi-squared test but the data you have do not come from two different populations (men vs. women), but actually come from the same people before and after a treatment, then we suggest you use a slightly different test. We would use a matched paired T-test and a McNemar Chi-squared test. If this is the case, then we would need to talk to a statistician to make sure we do this test correctly. These tests should also be done if we have matched pairs of people, namely a treatment group and a control group matched for age, sex and so on.

Analysis of costs

Analysing the cost of treatments is a more specialised type of quantitative analysis. In cost-effectiveness analysis, we basically calculate the cost of a treatment (cost evaluation) compared with the cost of other treatments and compare the difference between the two treatments with the differences in the benefits they achieve.

For example, one analgesic may cost £30 per approved dose and secures a reduction in pain score of 50 per cent within four hours, while another may cost £10 and secures a reduction in pain score of 40 per cent within four hours. The difference in costs between the analgesics is £20 while the difference in effect is a greater reduction in pain of 10 percentage points – which translates into £2 per percentage point reduction in pain. The question which needs to be asked is whether this is worth it?

However, the information above only relates to the actual acquisition cost of the analgesics. If the cheaper analgesic had a greater adverse event profile or incurred additional administration costs, then the total cost associated with its use might be significantly greater – say, for example, £50. In this case, it would be more expensive by £20 and less effective – a situation described as dominant, where one treatment is more effective and less expensive.

However, for evaluations involving a health economics component it is worth consulting a health economist, or for those who are interested to read the references at the end of this chapter.

In summary

- Qualitative data should be transcribed.
- Codes can be attached to ideas that emerge from reading the transcript.
- These codes can be used to develop themes.
- The themes can be brought together to give a general idea of what people report and we can support what we summarise with quotes as examples.
- When using quantitative data (numbers) always ask the advice of a statistician or someone experienced in quantitative analysis.
- Parametric tests are used on data that come from a sample with a normal distribution.
- Non-parametric tests are used on data that do not have a normal distribution.
- We use a T-test for comparing two means; we use a Chi-squared test for comparing two proportions.
- We use Pearson's correlation to look at the relationship between data that are normally distributed; we use Spearman's rank order correlation to look at the relationship between ordered data.
- We should get the advice of a health economist before undertaking any cost analysis. The health economics should be involved in the design, collection and planning of the data, not just brought in for the analysis.
- We can examine costs (cost evaluation) and we can compare these costs for treatments with similar outcomes (cost minimisation evaluation), or we can examine the cost per unit of benefit (cost effectiveness and cost utility evaluations).

Frequently asked questions

How do I know I've chosen the right codes?

This is always a difficult question, but realising that even the most experienced researchers struggle with it can be a comfort. The best way to code items is in terms of the questions you are trying to answer, so if we choose our example of the benefits or costs of a clinic, we will choose codes that can be related to identifying the benefits and costs of the clinic. We have to keep these in mind throughout our coding so that if an item comes up in the transcript that can be related to either the costs or benefits of the clinic, we can make sure we have coded that item and can include it in our final answering of the questions which were set at the outset of the evaluation.

What is the first step in data analysis – should I try to answer my primary evaluation question first?

No, the first step is to 'clean' your data (see Chapter 8) and to describe the sample. If you look at your sample and find out it is not representative of the population, then this will change the primary evaluation question, or at least it will change its interpretation and generalisability.

I have some concerns that, due to a low response rate, my sample may not be fully representative of the population I wish to generalise to – does this mean I can't carry out any statistical analysis?

You need to look at the sample and look at the non-responders. We need to know what the problem is with the non-responders, and who we are missing. If we know that we are missing the young or the most ill, then we can incorporate this into the interpretation of our findings. We can always carry out the analysis, but need to make it clear that these results are only representative of (for example) retired, white women with minor injuries, and do not reflect the general population of people attending the emergency department. It is then the reader's opinion as to how useful this is and if it is of any value. Ideally, we should try to improve the response rate to make it more representative and generalisable, if we have the time and money. This is where indicators are useful (see Chapter 4) – we will know early on if we have a problem in our response rate and so can do something about it as the evaluation is being undertaken and not wait until the end.

When I compared proportions across my two groups, there seems to be a difference, but the p value is 0.55 – how should I report this?

This might show a trend of one being different from the other. The sample size may have been too small to find a significant difference. Either more numbers are needed in the current study, or a further study with larger numbers is required. This suggests a trend towards one group but does not give a definitive answer that one group has more than the other group.

I've done some analysis but come up with some unexpected results that don't look right – what can I do about this?

Check your data (did you carry out data input checks?). Are there any results that might contain errors? Check the data have been entered correctly. Check your analysis. Ask someone else to repeat the analysis. Talk to other members of your team as to why these findings might have occurred. Think about why they are unexpected – did you make assumptions about what you would find that were incorrect?

Further reading

D. Altman (2005) *Statistics with Confidence.* London: BMJ Books.

A. Coffey and P. Atkinson (1996) *Making Sense of Qualitative Data: Complementary research strategies.* Thousand Oaks, CA: Sage.

A. Coffey, B. Holbrook and P. Atkinson (1996) 'Qualitative data analysis: technologies and representations', *Sociological Research Online.* 1(1), www.socresonline.org.uk/socresonline/1/1/4.html

B. Kirkwood and J. Sterne (2003) *Medical Statistics.* Oxford: Blackwell. Cost effectiveness:

David Silverman (1993) *Interpreting Qualitative Data: Methods for analysing talk, text and interaction.* Thousand Oaks, CA: Sage.

Cost effectiveness:

M.F. Drummond, B. O'Brien, G.L. Stoddart and G.W. Torrance (1997) *Methods for the Economic Evaluation of Health Care Programmes.* Oxford: Oxford Medical Publications.

T. Jefferson, V. Demicheli and M. Mugford (2000) *Elementary Economic Evaluation in Health Care*. London: BMJ Books.

P.R. McCrone (1998) *Understanding Health Economics: A guide for health care decision makers*. London: Kogan Page.

C.J. Phillips (2005) *Health Economics: An introduction for health professionals*. Oxford: Blackwell/BMJ Books.

Web pages

http://helios.bto.ed.ac.uk/bto/statistics/tress1.html#THE%20REALLY%20EASY%20STATISTICS%20SITE

http://bmj.bmjjournals.com/collections/statsbk/index.shtml

Pages to do statistics tests (please use with a statistician): http://statpages.org/

Cost effectiveness:

www.jr2.ox.ac.uk/bandolier/painres/download/whatis/Cost-effect.pdf
www.evidence-based-medicine.co.uk/What_is_series.html

10 Interpreting the Findings

Putting findings in context

The summary and presentation of findings will be influenced by the audience we are addressing. For example, reporting findings for sponsors of the work or senior managers/policy makers will emphasise different things than a summary for a patient newsletter would. Therefore, our report of conclusions and recommendations will need to be adjusted in light of our audience. However, the single most important thing is that any interpretation must be based on the results presented. Interpretations cannot be made about ideas that the evaluation did not examine or for which there are no results.

Involving the evaluation team in interpreting findings

The team we have put together at the outset of the study to agree aims, objectives, and methods can contribute again when the first results emerge. The team will include people with difference perspectives, skills and experiences, and interpretation of findings is strengthened considerably by consultation with team members at this stage.

It is useful to hold a meeting where the first layer of analysis is discussed. Inevitably this will raise questions as well as focus the evaluators back onto the original agreed aims and objectives. We will always find that we need to carry out several levels of analysis – each layer bringing further questions to be answered. For instance, in order to understand our results we will need to look at the characteristics of the groups – were they similar? And in what respects? Once we have carried out the main analyses against the primary evaluation questions, further questions will emerge, for example, about subsets of the data, or our understanding of unusual findings (please see FAQs, Chapter 9).

It is good practice to carry out the basic analysis and present these results to the Steering or Advisory Group so that the range of people involved in the evaluation can have the opportunity to comment on initial findings and raise queries or suggest further analysis that would be helpful.

Qualitative findings

Identify responses that relate to questions we are asking: It is clear that if we have asked people questions about some aspect of a service or intervention, then when we write our final report we need to present the answers to those questions in a way which makes sense and is related to the overall evaluation. If we are interested in the quality of a patient's experience of a visit to a rapid access chest pain clinic, then we have to decide which of the patient's answers to our questions are actually about the quality of their experience. So if a patient tells us that they found waiting to be seen in a noisy waiting room made them feel more ill, this is clearly something we will want to know about and report.

Interpretation should be directly related to the aims of the evaluation: Interpreting qualitative data is about deciding what is relevant to our evaluation aims and objectives and what is not. If, for example, someone had reported that a dog was barking outside the waiting room and that this had caused them some distress, this is less likely to be something we would want to include in our report to hospital managers as they are unlikely to be able to do anything about a one-off situation like a dog barking – of course, we might need to ascertain that the waiting room was not located near a dog pound, in which case it might be possible to arrange for better sound insulation or an alternative waiting room.

Views of different groups: It is also important to be able to distinguish between the views of different groups when we interpret our findings; for example, if we have recorded people's ethnic backgrounds we might discover that some groups' experiences are greatly affected by the gender of the person who examines them. It would be important to note this and make sure that it was identified as one of the factors that could influence the quality of patient experience. In the same way we might want to identify whether patients tell us they would prefer a translator to attend the clinic – the topic of the evaluation will dictate the priorities and relevance in any particular case. It is important to be careful not to attempt to make generalisations from findings from a small number of participants in this kind of study. Rather, the range of views can be captured to give an overall understanding of relevant factors, perhaps to be further explored in a larger study in order to understand how many people hold the various views.

Making interpretation more objective: It is impossible to achieve complete 'objectivity'. The wording of questions in questionnaires, decisions around sampling and all of the stages and processes are influenced by values and personal experience. That is why it is important to be clear about the processes involved in making the decisions which inform the research. Interpreting the findings is improved by having clarity around the decisions we make and good communication between researchers. For example, if two researchers are involved in coding, then they might go through their codes together and check that they agree. A discussion between them at the outset means that they can both agree on how things are coded (for example, are comments about the toilets coded under the patient experience or under the physical environment of the clinic?).

It is good to put the coding frame in an appendix and provide a detailed description of the ways in which the analysis sessions were undertaken with other researchers to improve 'inter-rater reliability'. It is never possible to be completely objective in research, but it is always possible to provide the grounds on which decisions and claims about the way the research has been carried out have been made.

In summary: Interpreting qualitative data is primarily about understanding the purposes of the evaluation and linking what our respondents have told us, or what we have observed with these purposes, in a sensible way that ensures that what we have learned from the data is communicated to the readers of the report. It can be very useful to identify some short extracts from interviews (properly anonymised, of course) which can illustrate the points we are presenting and to code these extracts when we are doing our analysis in a way that allows us to find them easily when we come to write our final report.

Quantitative Research

Cause and association

If one thing changes with another (the more food we eat, the more full we feel), then we would say they are associated. However, just because two things are associated does not mean we can make the interpretation that one causes the other. For example, a study conducted in South Africa[1] showed that there were significantly more storks flying in South African airspace in the early 1990s. The rise in stork sightings was perfectly correlated with the increase in newborn babies in South Africa

Cause and association

---

[1]M. Whitefield (1999) Do stories bring babies? Birth statistics in a South African health district in 1998, *South African Medical Journal*, 89 (9): 920–21.

during the same period, so this was cited as proof that storks deliver babies. This tongue-in-cheek report illustrates that just because one thing is associated and even perfectly correlated with another, it does not mean one causes the other.

The explanation for this is that often two things are associated because they are linked through another cause. For example, alcohol consumption used to be associated with lung cancer. Alcohol itself does not cause lung cancer, but people who drink regularly (in a pub) often smoke, and smoking may be the cause of lung cancer. This is called confounding (confounding means confusing, and in this case the link with smoking is confusing the association of alcohol and lung cancer).

The best way to find out whether one thing is caused by another is to do a randomised control trial (RCT). In an RCT, people are randomly allocated to the intervention or control group and therefore there shouldn't be any difference between people in each group, the only difference is in the treatment received. Any differences between groups in outcomes can therefore more confidently be attributed to the treatment itself. However, with interventions like smoking, it is not ethical to make people smoke or feasible to stop people smoking. Therefore, for studies where it is not possible to do a trial, then there needs to be other ways of showing cause. Sir Austin Bradford Hill suggested a set of seven points in order to establish cause:

1. There needs to be a strong relationship between a risk factor and the disease. Weak relationships may be due to chance or due to confounding. For example, the link between smoking and lung cancer is a stronger relationship than that between drinking alcohol and lung cancer.
2. There should be evidence that exposure to the risk factor precedes the start of the disease. For example, the people with lung cancer should have started smoking before they developed the cancer. If there are people who have developed cancer and then started smoking, this weakens the argument that smoking *causes* lung cancer.
3. There should be a reasonable biological explanation. That is, we should have a good reason for how and why a risk factor causes the disease.
4. The association should be repeated in other studies. If we can repeat the association with different populations and different study designs, this reduces the argument that the association is due to chance.
5. If the cause is removed, then we should see less of the disease. So, for example, if we can stop people smoking we should see less lung cancer.
6. There should be evidence of a dose response relationship. That is, the more cigarettes a person smokes, their higher their risk of developing lung cancer.
7. There should be no convincing alternative explanation of the cause of the disease.

In summary: We cannot generally conclude that one thing has caused another if we have done an observational study. We can just say that two things are associated. The level of evidence from an observational study (see Chapter 2 for Hierarchy of evidence) is not high enough to show cause, unless we can fulfil the list of seven indicators of probable cause – and this takes many studies and often many years. It is unlikely that such evidence will be produced from a local small-scale evaluation. In this type of study, appropriate control groups are often not in place, and random allocation to treatment group is even rarer. Comparisons should therefore only be made with caution, and the limitations of the study design should be acknowledged. In particular, association should not be interpreted as causation without meeting the seven criteria listed above.

Observation without a control group

If we give people a new drug for back pain and find out that five in ten people were completely free of back pain after two weeks, is this good? The answer is we don't know, because we have no idea how many people would have been free from back pain if we had done nothing. If we had done nothing we might find out that seven in ten people are free from back pain, so actually our drug is damaging and prolongs the

A control group

back pain. Without a control or the knowledge of what happens with the alternative treatment, we have no idea if our intervention is good. For example, if we introduce a new midwife-led birthing unit and find there are fewer caesareans after the unit is introduced than before the unit was in place (this is a 'before and after' study), the real reason for the reduction in caesareans might be other changes in the health care system. There might also have been a new policy introduced that is aimed at cutting the number of caesareans from 25 per cent down to 15 per cent of all births. So perhaps the number of caesareans would have decreased irrespective of the introduction of the birthing unit. To examine the effects of the unit we need to have compared it with a control hospital that is exposed to the same political pressures but does not have the new birthing unit.

In summary: It is useful if we can include a control group in order for us to be able to interpret and explain the data. If we do not have a control group, then we have to be very careful in our reporting. We can state that (for example) the caesarean rate decreased: this is a fact and an observation. However, we cannot state *why* this has happened. We will need to discuss the possible reasons; one reason might be the influence of the midwife-led birthing unit, another might be a change in policy, another might be a scare in the media regarding caesareans. The important thing is that we discuss the possible reasons and admit that we cannot conclude which of these caused the change we observed in caesarean rates. With a control group we can suggest it is less likely to be due to media and policy and more likely to be due to the new midwife-led unit. Without a control group we cannot suggest a cause but can discuss a range of possible causes.

The Hawthorne effect

Hawthorne effect

The Hawthorne effect is the idea that if you are studying something you change it. For example, if I tell people I am looking at exercise levels and I send everyone a questionnaire about how much exercise they have done in the past week, just by asking them about exercise I will make them think about exercise and so make them actually do more exercise. I might send them an exercise video and then some questionnaires about how much exercise they have done. I would then think that my video is great and increases everyone's exercise levels. Therefore, I should sell my video. However, it could turn out that no one actually watched my video. That the repeated questionnaires reminded people to do exercise and that is what got them to raise their exercise levels. Therefore, the act of studying people can make their behaviour change. When doing our evaluation we need to interpret things carefully if there is a possibility that the study itself could have caused the effects seen.

In summary: If we are doing an intervention we need to acknowledge the Hawthorne effect, or account for it by perhaps having a control/ comparison group who also are exposed to the Hawthorne effect but not the intervention.

Interpretation based on evidence

When we come to a conclusion it is vital that we base our conclusions on the evidence we have actually found. Look at Case 10.1 and see if these are limitations to this study that need to be acknowledged in the interpretion.

CASE STUDY 10.1

Evaluation of a one day mental health course

Aims: An evaluation of a one day (8 hour) course.

Participants: Target audience – people providing services for people with mental illness.

Methods: A questionnaire was completed by all participants before, after and at a three month follow-up. This evaluation was conducted using all the participants from the 2003 courses.

Results: Questionnaires were completed by 114 (69 per cent) of participants on all three occasions (n=165). The responses showed a significant increase in self-assessed knowledge and confidence in dealing with people with mental health disorders, and this effect lasted until the three month assessment. Participants were largely positive before entering the course in their attitude to people with mental health problems and this did not change significantly three months post course.

Conclusions: The mental health course was successful in improving confidence and knowledge regarding providing services for people with mental health problems.

Source: adapted from P. Grootemaat et al. (2006) Working together for mental health: evaluation of a one-day mental health course for human service providers. *BMC Psychiatry*; 6 (1): 50.

Question: Is the interpretation justified? What else would you like to know before agreeing with this conclusion?

Summarising and presenting data

A real help to interpreting the data is to summarise these in tables and graphs. This helps us make sense of the data. Excel and other software packages are very useful for making graphs and charts, so drawing the charts is not difficult, but we need to understand what we are drawing.

The basic rules to follow are:

- Always give a title to all tables and graphs.
- Always put the units on the axis of the graph or in the header of the table.
- Always give the source of the data.

Tables

Tables are for giving a summary of the data, so they should be simple and easy to follow. We don't want just a printout of our spreadsheet and we don't want something cluttered and complicated. Tables should be clear and easy to understand at a glance. The advantage of a table is that real numbers can be seen and they are much easier than a long bit of text, but quite often it can be hard to see trends. Figure 10.1 gives examples of the same data in different formats.

Text

The change in fatigue levels with treatment showed that men changed from a baseline score of 9 (scale 0–10) to an end of study score of 6, giving a total change of -3 units over the duration of the study. Women changed from a baseline score of 8 (scale 0–10) to an end-of-study score of 3, giving a total change of -5 units over the duration of the study.

Table

Change in fatigue score with treatment.

(Continued)

(Continued)

	Baseline fatigue score (0–10 scale)	End of study fatigue score (0–10 scale)
Male	9	6
Female	8	3

Graph

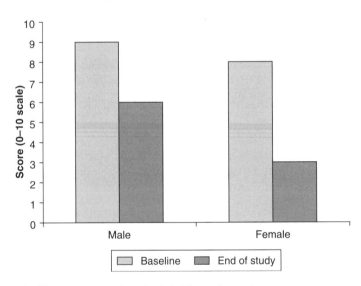

Figure 10.1   Data presented as test, table and graph

Graphs

Graphs are very good at getting over a message visually. They have a great impact if they are kept very simple and focused. Generally the vertical axis (y axis) is for the data that we are interested and the horizontal axis (x axis) is for the data that we think changes the data we are interested in. For example, how has the number of new cases of flu changed with time? We would put dates on the bottom axis (x axis) and cases for flu on the vertical (y axis). How does fatigue level change with age? We would put ages on the bottom (x axis) and fatigue levels on the vertical (y axis).

Keep it very simple; don't try to put too much data in a graph. The various types of graph (see Figure 10.2) are:

- **Line graphs** are used to show data over a time period. They are used for data that are continuous.
- **Bar charts** are used to show numbers or groups of people who fit certain categories. A bar graph is a fast way of seeing differences within groups at a glance.

- **Scattergrams** are used to explore the data and show correlations.
- **Pie charts** show proportions or percentages.

Line graph:

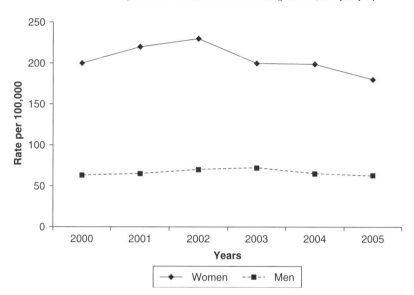

Bar chart:

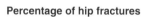
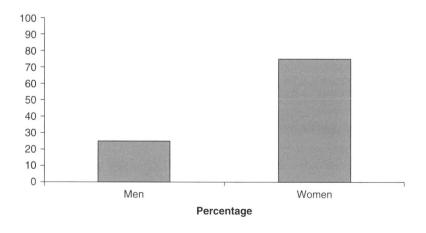

Scattergram:

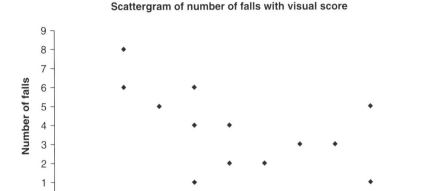

Pie chart:
Last address of patients attending hospital for fracture.

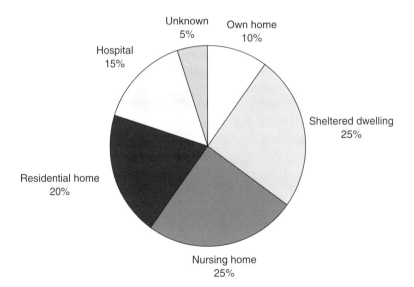

Figure 10.2   Various types of graph

Practise your tables and graphs

Now work out the presentation of the following:

1. Proportion of smokers by those with lung cancer compared to those without lung cancer.
2. Number of cases of measles occurring in the country over the past ten years.
3. Demographic data (age, sex, disease duration, housing type, etc) about the people replying to a survey.

4. On the pie chart in Figure 10.2, where did most people live before going into hospital?
5. In Figure 10.2, what is wrong with the bar chart?

Answers:

1. Bar chart.
2. Line graph.
3. Table.
4. Sheltered dwellings and nursing homes.
5. There is no label on the y axis, and the x axis is labelled incorrectly. The number of patients we are talking about should also be given. The source of the data is missing as well.

Frequently asked questions

I have carried out the analysis that we planned at the outset, but I now find that several other questions have emerged – can I do additional analyses to look at these questions?

You can, but you need to be very careful. This is called data mining or fishing. Just looking at the data to see things that you hadn't thought of before is interesting and can give ideas for new research, but the results cannot be taken too strongly:

(a) The study might be designed but not have enough people to find a difference related to the other questions, so we might report something is not related when if fact we did not have enough people (the power) to find this difference.

(b) The p value (significance test) tells me the chance that I have found something interesting. It is based on the idea that if I do 100 analyses, five will appear significant by chance (see Chapter 7, Understanding Data). If I do 20 tests, one will be significant by chance (5/100 = 20 per cent). So the more tests I do, the more likely I will get significant results by chance. Therefore fishing around in the data doing interesting extra questions and analyses runs the risk of finding something 'significant' which is just an error and a chance occurrence due to a variation in samples.

I have been asked to present our evaluation results to senior managers within my organisation but I have only just started the analysis and am not very confident of the results – should I present findings at this stage?

No, not unless you have to; there is no point giving people results that might be wrong. If you need time to understand the evaluation better and to repeat analysis to be sure of your findings, you should not present these. Presenting it too early may mean you mislead people. Senior mangers may leave the meeting ready to implement changes based on your wrong or inaccurate findings. Then you will have to come back later when you have made the analysis and are confident, and tell them you got it wrong because it was at an early stage. If you have not finished, don't present the findings as they are likely to give the wrong impression and message. You need time to interpret findings, think about their generalisability, the limitations of the study, discuss with others, repeat some analysis, and generally understand the meaning of findings before presenting anything.

The commissioners of my evaluation would like to see that the new service comes out favourably but I am not sure that my findings will be very positive – what should I do?

You should report accurately and base the findings on the evidence from the evaluation. You can try to put the best light on these when interpreting, but everything should be based on the evidence and findings of the evaluation. If something does not work and you try to show it does, you are going to be doing a disservice to patients and the organisation. You will be encouraging people to direct time, money and resources to something that you know does not work, instead of helping to develop something better that does work.

I would like to involve members of the advisory group in interpreting my findings but I don't have much time – would it be OK to just include them when I circulate a first draft for comments?

Unfortunately that is what most people end up doing, but it is not very good practice. The advisory group will be affected by your interpretations being already applied; you will not get such a range of ideas and inputs in your report as people can really only comment on what you have written and will be very limited in the input they can give personally in the way things are written. Interpretation should be a team effort and not the views of one person in a hurry.

Further reading

C. Seale, G. Gobo, J.F. Gubrium and D. Silverman (eds) (2007) *Qualitative Research Practice.* London: Sage.

Web pages
www.mcwdn.org/Graphs/BarGraph.html
www.emro.who.int/rpc/pdf/healthresearchers_guide.pdf

11 Writing a Report

What is a report?

A report is the way of publishing and circulating the findings and recommendations of an evaluation. It is usually requested by the funders and so they will often specify how they want the report written. A report is a way of communicating the results of the evaluation and providing evidence from your study. Generally, this is the way many business or government departments disseminate the findings of evaluations and other investigations.

Some types of reports

There are many different types of reports and they all have their own conventional structure. For example, annual reports, progress reports, feasibility reports, student project reports, accident reports, laboratory reports, appraisal reports, audit reports, and scientific reports. We need to know what type of report we will be writing so that we know how it should be organised.

Basic things to think about before writing the report

- Reports are always highly structured and follow conventions that are generally set up by the organisation commissioning the evaluation or asking for the report. We can get an idea of how the report should look if we get the terms of reference or a copy of a report that someone else has written for this organisation. We can then follow the guidelines and use the previous successful report as a template in designing our report.
- We need to think about the audience. What is the reader expecting from this report? What is the purpose of writing it and who is our target audience? What does the audience already know and what do they want to

know? What is the most important thing for our readers to understand from the evaluation? The report should be written with a very clear idea of the target audience.

- We should make a plan or outline of the report. We can put in the headings and then a few lines or notes to ourselves of what will go in each section. Reports do require careful planning; their presentation needs to be logical and clear. So we need to write an outline structure of the report and then build on this with different drafts.

Update the date every time we amend the report

- We can try to write alongside data collection and analysis. We can write the methods section quite early on and do a first draft of the background and introduction. Ideally, writing the methods section as we actually carry out the evaluation means we don't forget anything. If we can get a few lines down on paper then it makes starting the report writing easier. It can be very hard to get on with writing the report and can be easy to put it off until the end, when it is likely to be an enormous task. If we start early on, we can get on with the writing part and can come back and improve it later.

- We will need to come back and re-write sections of the report, as well as include comments from partners, so we will need to keep track of which draft we are working on. 'Version control' is very important. Put a date on the report and update this every time you amend you report.

- The timetable and plan we had for the evaluation should include a period for report writing.

- Make a list of all the people who contributed to the evaluation and so could be involved in writing the report and find a way to allow everyone to contribute what they need to. We should not try to write the report alone.

Writing up

Outline structure of the report

Reports need to be very clearly structured. Readers will not want a book but they will want to find the main things they are looking for where they expect to find them. Lots of people will not read the report from cover to cover but will read the summary and then skip to the end and read the recommendations – they might even look at the methods! Therefore, we need to have a very clear structure so that any reader can find what they are looking for. A report is meant to be scanned quickly. Here are some components of a typical report structure:

Cover sheet: This includes the full title of the report, our name, name of the unit where the evaluation was undertaken, name of institution, date.

Title page: This contains the full title of the report. We should include keywords in the title that might help people when searching the literature.

Table of contents: This lays out the headings and subheadings used in the report with their page numbers. For example, the first chapter will be Chapter 1 and sections within this might be 1.1, 1.2 and so on. Subsections of these parts would be 1.1.1, 1.1.2 and so on.

Each section and subsection should be listed with the relevant page number. Diagrams and tables can be listed separately under 'List of figures' together with the page numbers where they appear. A typical report might be structured like this:

Executive summary: This is an overview of the whole report. It should show the reader in advance what is in the report. This section should summarise the aims, methods, main findings and conclusions. The summary should be short, normally only 150–200 words. This means people normally write the executive summary last, when they have a very clear and focused idea of the main emphasis of the report. The summary is one of the most important parts of the report, as this is the only bit that many people will read. It should be used to 'sell' our report to others. The summary should give a clear if limited understanding of the main findings and conclusions.

Body of the report

Literature review/background: This puts the evaluation in context and explains its importance in relation to what others have done before and what is already known. The length of this section will be determined by the type of readers we expect. If they already know a great deal we might not need a lot of explanation, we might just need to set our aims in context. In general we want to give the purpose, context and a feel for the previous work in this field.

Aims and objectives: What the purpose of the work is (aims) and what it sets out to achieve (objectives). What the most important feature of the evaluation is.

Methods: This is an explanation of methods, the materials used, the people included and excluded, and includes how and when the evaluation was done. A report on ethical issues (that is, was ethical approval granted?) should also be presented. This section should be written so clearly that another person should be able to duplicate exactly the evaluation elsewhere, using just this section. It can be divided up into sections to include evaluation design, participants, techniques and equipment, sequence of events, data collected, data analysis and so on.

Findings/results: This is a clear presentation of the results. This section simply states and presents the actual results of the study. It should be structured so that it directly flows from the aims and objectives. It should not discuss the meaning or interpretation but simply present results. Tables, graphs and other forms of illustrating the results are normally included here. However, figures should supplement the findings given. We don't need to describe in the text something that is in a figure or in a table; this is a waste of time and space. We might give the main 'take-home' message from the table but we should not duplicate information in the text that can be found in the tables and graphs. All the figures should be self-contained and labelled correctly. A reader should be able to look at a table or graph and understand it without reading the text. This is the section where we will also present findings from our qualitative data, and here we can include quotes from participants which illustrate particular points we are making. The first paragraph in this section should describe the population and should give us an idea of the structure (demographics) of the sample: the age and sex of responders compared to non-responders, and any other relevant details for us to understand if this sample is representative.

Discussion/comment: This section explains the meaning of the results and gives our interpretation of the findings. We should examine how the findings compare with other evaluations done in this area. What limitations or alternative explanations are there for the findings? We should highlight any limitations of the study, both those that have arisen from the design or from results (for example, any missing data). Importantly, the analysis and discussion can only be based on our results. There should not be any new results presented in this section – and all points raised should be based on results presented in the previous chapter. We should not include opinions but should just comment on the evidence from our evaluation and discuss the implications for practice or policy.

Conclusions: This is a brief summary of the main findings. This section should be short and should not introduce any new ideas. We should be able to tie in the aims and objective to the answers given in the conclusions. However, we cannot draw conclusions that are not backed up by the findings or by our evidence. We will need to support all our conclusions with the data we have drawn up from our evaluation. We can simply state the evidence-based interpretations, but we cannot make judgements or recommendations in this section.

Recommendations: This is a brief section where we can make suggestions for further action or what should happen in the future. This is where we talk about how our evaluation fits in with general work in the field. It is a demonstration of the importance and implications of our findings.

References: These are all the relevant sources that we have used in our report.

Appendix: This is where we can put in any information that is relevant to the report but which needs to be kept separate to avoid interrupting the development of the main body of the report. We might include a copy of the questionnaires used. We might also include photographs or extra data that might benefit the report but are not essential for the understanding of the evaluation. Anything can be placed in an appendix as long as it is relevant and there is a reference to it in the main body of the report. Place appendices in order of where they appear in the main body of the report. So Appendix 1 (the questionnaire) might come first, then Appendix 2 (interview schedule) and so on.

Some other sections that can be included in a report but are not always essential are:

List of abbreviations and/or Glossary: This is an alphabetical list of the abbreviations that might not be familiar to the reader.

Acknowledgements: A short paragraph thanking any person or organisation that has helped with the work.

In summary: Reports need to present the data very clearly and concisely. The information needs to be put in a place where the reader expects to find it. We do not want new findings given in the conclusions or in the discussion. Nor do we want findings to be given in the executive summary that are not mentioned in the main body of the report. A report has to be consistent and logical. It is to give information and is not an essay or an argument.

Presentation and style

- We should use a consistent voice in the report. For example, a passive voice is 'It is recommended', or 'Analysis was undertaken'. An active voice is 'We recommend', or 'We undertook analysis of'. If we are using one voice in the report, we should not change this during the writing. We need to be consistent.
- All the headings and separate sections should stand out clearly.
- Formatting should be consistent and clear.
- We should always get someone else to proofread and check the spelling.

Use the report checklist given in Figure 11.1 to help ensure that nothing has been overlooked.

Time for report writing included in the evaluation plan.	
Have identified a team of people involved in writing the report.	
Copy of guidelines from the organisation which has commissioned the report.	
Clear idea of why we are writing the report and who are the target audience.	
Explanation of all unfamiliar or technical terms.	
Pages numbered.	
Title is accurate and reflects the major emphasis of the report.	
Date added to report so that re-drafts do not become confused.	
Contents page complete and lists all main sections with the right page number.	
Sample size given (where relevant).	
Methods directly related to aims.	
Discussion directly related to results detailed in the report.	
Limitation of report discussed (bias, lost to follow-up, small samples and so on).	
Executive summary is understood by others.	
Spell check and grammar check completed.	
Tables and diagrams clearly labelled.	
There is a reference in the text to all the tables and graphs.	
Proof reading by someone else.	
Illustrations used are not subject to copyright.	
All members of the team have read and agree with the report.	
Abbreviations are explained.	
Additional information in clearly labelled appendices.	

Figure 11.1   Report checklist

Dissemination: writing for publication

We can disseminate our work in several ways – it is possible to put reports (as pdf files so that they cannot be altered) on a website, for instance that of the organisation where the work took place. Abstracts of the work can be submitted to conferences for oral or poster presentation, where people working in a similar field are likely to be in the audience to discuss findings. Or, to reach the widest possible audience, we can consider publishing in a relevant scientific journal.

We always aim to carry out evaluation – of any scale – to the standards that are required by journals that publish peer-reviewed articles. This helps ensure that our work is robust and that readers can be confident about the trustworthiness of our results. As we have explained, this means taking care at all stages of the study to work to an explicit protocol (that everyone is following), for literature searching, sampling, data collection and the analysis of data. Even though in local, small-scale evaluation it is usually neither a requirement nor a priority to publish findings, we believe that following such standards throughout a study – including at write-up stage – leads to stronger evaluations, giving confidence to local practitioners and policy makers to act on such findings. Although the purpose of a study may not have been to generate generalisable evidence, there may often be messages that are applicable to a wider audience, and that may be felt to be useful to inform practice more widely. In this case, we may seek to publish our findings in an academic journal. It may be helpful to consult with people who have experience of publishing their work, but some simple, general rules apply to writing for publication:

- Identify the primary aim of the paper and stick to this aim throughout – do not include background material, methods or results that fall outside this one aim. Generally a paper needs to be more tightly defined than an evaluation report. You need to be clear about the 'story' or 'hook' for the paper, and write to that.
- Identify an appropriate journal for the paper and follow the guidelines for that journal.
- Think about who reads that journal and ensure that your paper addresses their interests and concerns.
- Ensure that your methods are clear and fully described.
- Consult an appropriate expert – perhaps a statistician, health economist or qualitative researcher – before submitting your paper.
- Expect to be turned down once or twice before achieving your goal – believe in your work and use reviewers' comments to strengthen your paper.

For further guidance about writing for publication, see the BMJ's website guidance for authors at http://resources.bmj.com/bmj/authors?resource_name=Authors

Summary

- Reports follow a very clear structure.
- The target audience is very important in deciding what should go into a report. As you are writing always think about the reader.
- It is important to get guidelines from the funding organisation or an example of a previous successful report to act as a template to writing the report.
- Most reports have: a contents page, executive summary, background and aims, methods, findings, discussion, conclusion, recommendations, references and appendix.
- The results should clearly reflect the aims.

- The conclusions should come directly from the results.
- The discussion should be centred around the results of the evaluation and put them in context.
- Standards required for publication should be followed in order to produce the most robust and convincing write-up – this will lead to work that is most likely to be used to influence practice.

Frequently asked questions

As people who read reports are generally busy, wouldn't it be better to leave out the detail of methods to avoid wasting people's time?

No, people can only decide if they believe your findings if they know what you did. There are always different ways of doing things, so other people might want to know what you did in order to repeat you evaluation in their own locality; they will want to know your methods in order to understand the meaning of the findings. The methods are one of the most important sections in the whole report.

In the results chapter it is quite frustrating to not discuss what the results mean – why does this need to be left until the discussion chapter?

Results should be factual, a true representation of what has been found. They should not be opinion based. However, discussion is about interpreting findings and putting them in context, so they are opinion based. When reading a report we will want to know what has been found and which bits are the opinion and interpretation of the writer. We might disagree with the discussion but we should not be able to disagree with the results, as they are just what happened and not opinion based.

Since we carried out our evaluation, another study has been undertaken locally with results that are relevant to our work – can I include these results alongside ours?

Yes, if they complement each other and you can describe the other study's methods well, then it is better to give a bigger picture. As long as the other evaluation is transparent and is relevant then yes, they can be presented and contrasted with each other.

Analysis has taken longer than we expected, and now writing up seems to be taking forever – are there are any short-cuts?

One short-cut can be to get different members of the team to draft different bits, so there is simultaneous writing of the report; try not to leave it all to one person. Another short-cut is to write some bits as you go along, such as the background section, and your methods can be written early on in the evaluation. This saves time later. To do this you can make a template and so fill out the relevant sections when you are able and not leave this to the end.

Our primary evaluation question has changed since we started the evaluation – how do I now write up my findings?

You need to say why the primary research question changed, what happened and what evidence there is that the question needed to change. Can you justify that you had the ability (numbers, design) to answer the new question even if the original design was set up to answer a different question? Basically, you need to justify the change in the primary evaluation question.

Our commissioners have asked us to report key findings before we have finished our analysis and this is difficult – what should I say?

You can report on things you do know – the methods, how many recruited, types of people participating, early trends and ideas. But you cannot report on things for which you do not have data or have not done any analysis; you should not report your hunches about what is happening. You need to put things in the correct context, and realise that these are early results and could be inaccurate. There will be no definitive answer because the analysis is not yet finished.

Further reading

John Bowden (2004) *Writing a Report: How to prepare, write and present effective reports.* Plymouth: How to Books.

Web pages
www.mdx.ac.uk/www/study/Reports.htm

CASE STUDY 11.1

Executive summary: An evaluation of a telemedicine service between primary and secondary care for minor orthopaedic conditions in Swansea

Background: A telemedicine link was set up between a GP surgery and the orthopaedic department of a nearby acute hospital, funded through the Welsh Assembly Government's Innovations in Care programme.

In this small-scale evaluation of the service, processes of care were described, patient satisfaction was assessed, and the views of the doctors providing the service were gathered.

Methods: Patients who presented to their GP with a designated minor orthopaedic condition that required further investigation with an orthopaedic consultant were offered a telemedicine consultation at their local surgery. Processes of care were tracked for all patients who consented to participate in the study over a seven-month period during 2002, and all participants were sent a follow-up questionnaire to assess their satisfaction with the service. Semi-structured interviews with GPs and an orthopaedic consultant were conducted. The interview schedule was developed from a literature review of the topic and discussions with local research colleagues. Interviews were piloted with a GP academic and all were taped, transcribed and analysed according to themes revealed.

Results: Seventy-nine patients were included in the study, with conditions including ganglia (n = 22), carpal tunnel syndrome (n = 9), and toe deformities (n = 11). Following their telemedicine consultation, 36 patients (46 per cent) were referred directly to day case surgery, eight (10 per cent) were put on the inpatient waiting list, six (7 per cent) were given self-care advice and two (3 per cent) were referred for an outpatient appointment. In 27 cases (34 per cent) other treatment or investigation was required, including steroid injection, x-ray and possible referral to different specialist, electromyography studies to confirm diagnosis, referral for MRI scan, continue current treatment, referral for nerve condition studies, physiotherapy, and soft spot insole in shoe.

Of 79 questionnaires sent out, 73 (84 per cent) were returned completed. Patients expressed high levels of satisfaction in general, and in particular with the time spent in consultation, the attention given to what the patient said, and the explanation of what was done (rated as 'excellent': 67 per cent, 65 per cent, 64 per cent, 68 per cent respectively). Some patients reported feeling anxious before (n = 22) or during (n = 11) the video consultation.

Four interviews were carried out, three with the participating GPs and one with the orthopaedic consultant. Views are presented in brief below, by theme:

- *Process*: All interviewees reported that they had found using the new equipment straightforward, once they had become used to it.
- *Environment*: GPs felt that a larger than average consulting room was needed, with a private area for changing.
- *Communication*: No difficulties were reported with carrying out the consultation over the link, and that being with the patient helped by providing an advocate for issues raised.
- *Time*: Appointments were set at alternating 10 and 15 minute intervals, which was felt to be appropriate. When patients failed to turn up, time was used for administration or a chat with the consultant. The study depended on additional GP and consultant sessions, although the respondents were clear that any future service would need to be integrated and extra sessions reimbursed.
- *Patient response*: GPs reported that patients were very positive about the new link.
- *Broader issues*: GPs were interested in how the telemedicine service could be expanded to other conditions or health professionals and for educational purposes.

Conclusions: Results were encouraging, with a majority of patients who undertook a telemedicine consultation avoiding a trip to the acute hospital for an appointment with the orthopaedic consultant. Most patients reported being very satisfied with the new service.

The GPs and consultant were generally positive about the video link for consultations, reporting that patients were happy with the service. They were keen to see the service develop, although they stressed the need for integration.

A comparison of processes, outcomes and costs with the usual care would be required, ideally in a randomised controlled trial, before the full impact of the service could be established.

Appendix I: Example of an Evaluation Report

An evaluation of a telemedicine service between primary and secondary care for minor orthopaedic conditions in Swansea.

1. Background:

Telemedicine is a broad term that describes medicine carried out at a distance. Clinical information is transmitted usually by electronic means and generally a patient is seeking information at one end from an expert at the other end. An example of this might be video-conferencing or telephone helplines. One of the key features of telemedicine is that it could increase accessibility to specialist health care for remote or rural area. Telemedicine has been used by the military [1, 2] and on board ambulances in Denmark and Wales to transmit ECGs to a remote hospital for the assessment of patients with suspected acute myocardial infarction [3, 4]. Many exciting things have been predicted for telemedicine in terms of revolutionising the way some areas of medicine could be performed. Evaluation studies have shown high levels of diagnostic accuracy [5] and high patient satisfaction [6].

1.1 Evaluation aim
To assess whether telemedicine consultations are an effective way of seeing patients for initial consultations with an orthopaedic surgeon for minor orthopaedic conditions in terms of process of care and the views of patients and clinical providers of the service.

1.2 Objectives
To:

1. Describe the processes of care associated with being treated in this way, such as use and uptake of the service.
2. Identify any difficulties associated with carrying out a consultation over the video link:

    i. problems with diagnosis;
    ii. communication difficulties.

3. Assess the satisfaction of patients who are seen by the consultant over the video link.
4. Gather the views of participating GPs and consultants concerning the use of the service and its potential for wider use.

1.3 Research setting

The telemedicine equipment was installed in the orthopaedic consultant's office in the orthopaedic department in the hospital and in a consulting room in a participating GP practice. The telemedicine equipment consisted of a large television screen, on top of which sat a small video camera. A key-pad was linked which controlled the camera and this was used to dial up the link. During a consultation the GP would demonstrate the patient's condition to the consultant showing the body part to the main camera and the consultant could instruct the GP to zoom in or out or adjust the focus to get the best image. After viewing the patient the consultant would decide on the next course of action, such as treatment or further investigation. Several practices in the area were able to refer patients for the telemedicine service, which was held every fortnight specifically for minor orthopaedic conditions (such as trigger finger, carpal tunnel decompression, ganglia or toe deformities).

2. Evaluation methods

All the patients taking part in the study gave written consent. The GPs were asked to fill in a data collection form for each patient to record basic patient data (age, sex, clinical condition). All patients who consented were sent a questionnaire to assess satisfaction. Interviews were conducted individually with each GP and the consultant. A semi-structured format was used. The aim of the interviews was to understand how they felt about carrying out the consultation over the video link. The interviews were recorded and transcribed and general themes identified by two independent researchers. A single telemedicine session was used as a pilot study to test the data collection forms, questionnaires and consent forms, and amendments were made following discussion with staff after this initial pilot session.

2.1 Arriving at themes for interviews

A review of the telemedicine literature was undertaken and identified a number of qualitative studies that included interviews with clinicians as part of their data collection procedure. These studies explored issues such as the ability to operate equipment, and the quality and resolution of images. These issues were considered when devising the interview schedule and were discussed with academic colleagues. As a result six topic areas became part of the interview schedule: process, environment, communication, time, patient response and broader issues.

2.2 Analysis of results

Quantitative data from the data collection forms and patient questionnaires were stored and analysed on SPSS v 11. Open-ended answers from the questionnaires and qualitative data were grouped and reported by theme, with quotes to illustrate the themes present.

3. Results

3.1 Patient recruitment

Twelve telemedicine sessions were held with 6–13 patient appointments in each session. Table 1 shows attendance and average time taken per session. The average time taken was 14.6 mins per patient with a range of 12.1–16.4 minutes. Of the 87 patients who attended, 79 consented to take part. Of these patients the mean age was 56 years (range 21–84 years), and 54 (62.1 per cent) were female. All 79 patients were sent a follow-up questionnaire and 73 (83 per cent) returned the questionnaire.

3.2 Outcomes of teleconsultations

The outcomes are shown in Table 2. In just under half of the consultations patients were referred for a day case surgery. The mean length of time people waited between their teleconsultation and surgery was 128 days, ranging from 51 to 269.

3.3 Patient satisfaction

Patients satisfaction levels were generally high, particularly so with the convenience of location of the surgery and with the time of the appointment, the length of time they had to wait, and the time spent in the consultations and their overall care (see Table 3). No problems were reported on hearing the specialist, most patients reported that they could talk to the specialist as well as face-to-face (n=66, 91.7 per cent). Overall, 86.1 per cent (n=62) reported they would have their consultation by video link again if given the choice and nine stated they would choose to go to hospital.

Several patients made comments about the teleconsultation and the value of having the consultation with the specialist with the GP present:

- 'Made me feel very relaxed and comfortable and able to discuss my problems' (M7049).
- 'I was impressed with the speed at which I was able to have a teleconsultation with the consultant. The consultation was clear, informative and a method that I felt at ease with' (K24215).
- 'The video link consultation is ideal; it gave me a great deal of comfort to know my own doctor was present. He could hear the specialist's comments, in my opinion it was excellent' (K22354).

3.4 Provider's views

3.4.1 the equipment and consulting room

Interviewees were asked about how they found operating the equipment and reported in general that it was straightforward:

- 'There was a learning curve initially, but once I got used to it, it has been straightforward' (Int D).

Table 1 Telemedicine sessions held during study period, and attendance

Session date	Number of appointments made inc. re-appointments	Number of appointments for which patients attended	Number of patient consultations completed	Duration of session (minutes)	Average time per patient (minutes)
22.4.02 (Pilot)	7	5	5	100	20.0
10.5.02	6	6	6	90	15.0
20.5.02	9	8	8	145	15.6
07.6.02	8	8	8	115	14.4
24.6.02	7	7	7	115	16.4
01.7.02	6	5	5	75	15.0
15.7.02	8	7	7	100	14.3
05.8.02	9	4	0	N/A	
19.8.02	9	7	7	105	15.0
07.10.02	13	12	12	145	12.1
21.10.02	10	6	6	75	12.5
04.11.02	10	9	9	120	13.3
Total	**102**	**84**	**80**	**1165**	**14.6**

Table 2   Outcome of teleconsultations

Patient disposition	Frequency	Per cent
Referral to day case surgery list	36	45.6
Put on inpatient waiting list	8	10.1
Self-care advice	6	7.6
Outpatient appointment required	2	2.5
Other treatment advised	12	15.2
Other	15	19.0
Total	**79**	**100.0**

Table 3   Patient satisfaction with processes of teleconsultation

Criteria rating (frequency of completion)	Excellent frequency (per cent)	Very good frequency (per cent)	Good frequency (per cent)	Fair frequency (per cent)	Poor frequency (per cent)
Length of time waited for appointment (n=71)	28(39.4)	26(36.6)	10(14.1)	5(7.0)	2(2.8)
Convenience of location of surgery (n=72)	41(56.9)	19(26.4)	10(23.6)	2(2.8)	–
Getting through to surgery by phone (n=39)	8(20.5)	14(35.9)	11(28.2)	3(7.7)	3(7.7)
Length of time waiting at surgery (n=71)	39(54.9)	25(35.2)	5(7.0)	1(1.4)	1(1.4)
Time spent in consultation (n=71)	46(64.8)	19(26.8)	5(7.0)	1(1.4)	–
Ease of making/ changing appointment time (n=19)	5(26.3)	7(36.8)	4(21.1)	2(10.5)	1(5.3)
Convenience of day/time of appointment (n=72)	39(54.2)	20(27.8)	11(15.3)	2(2.8)	–
Attention given to what patient said (n=72)	46(63.9)	20(27.8)	5(6.9)	1(1.4)	–
Explanation of what was done (n=72)	49(68.1)	16(22.2)	7(9.7)	–	–
Overall visit (n=72)	48(66.7)	17(23.6)	6(8.3)	1(1.4)	–

However, the consulting room was criticised:

- 'More game show than consultation, I think' (Int B).
- 'Occasionally somebody has come into the room, so perhaps one should block it off ...' (Int A).

3.4.2 communicating with patients and professionals

In terms of the dynamics between the people involved, there was a mixed response from professionals; there were feelings it might be easier on the patient, but is hard to gauge the patient's reaction at a distance:

- 'I think it is easier for the patient in some ways, you [the patient] have got an advocate helping you, in some ways expressing what your worries are, there are times where the patients have whispered a little off side to me and I was able to relay this to the consultant' (Int B).
- 'Normally I would draw diagrams for patients, for example, things like operations, and obviously you couldn't do that in the same way. I would draw on my pad and hold it up but I couldn't assess how well that came across' (Int D).
- 'When patients did not attend their appointments the usual pattern was: sit down and wait and talk to each other on the link, you can't shut the link down and go and do some paperwork; it might be better to over-book in some respects' (Int C).

3.4.3 broader issues

When asked about other uses of telemedicine, the interviewees were positive and remarked that there was great potential:

- 'Thinking about backs, we have a big problem, they are telling us that they can't see them for two years. If you had a session where you could prioritise them with basic history, then perhaps you could streamline referrals' (Int C).
- 'This would be an ideal way to conduct follow-ups after an operation, it would relieve the out-patients of a huge burden' (Int D).
- 'It's an excellent teaching tool because we are possibly going to arrange an injection session. We could sit in the surgery and have everything shown' (Int A).

3.5 Key findings

The main findings from the in-depth interviews are:

- The equipment was felt to be straightforward, with only teething problems reported around focussing the camera.
- Greater privacy was reported to be necessary for patients.
- GPs and consultants reported that there was good communication, efficient use of consultation time, and shorter waiting times.
- The GP presence provided benefit to the patients, with the role seen as that of a skilled advocate communicating with the consultant.
- There was a general sense of professional enjoyment and achievement.
- The was extensive potential for use of the service, including patient follow-up and education and training for various professional groups including GPs, nurses, physiotherapists and consultants.

4. Discussion

4.1 Summary of main evaluation findings

Of 102 appointments made, 80 (78 per cent) resulted in a completed consultation. Almost half of the patients seen by video link were able to be referred directly for day case surgery, avoiding a separate trip to the main hospital for an outpatient appointment. Of these, two-thirds had their surgery completed within the study period, waiting an average of 128 days. In general, patients reported very high levels of satisfaction with the service, with many enthusiastic comments made concerning the experience. However, a minority of patients reported feelings of anxiety and difficulties in communication. The clinicians were also, in general, enthusiastic about the service and its potential applications in the provision of a wider range of services and for training purposes. Equipment was reported to be simple to use and no difficulties were reported by the GPs or consultant in communicating over the link.

4.2 Study limitations

This small-scale study was set up as a local evaluation, and the study design did not allow conclusions to be drawn about the costs and benefits of the telemedicine service compared to the standard service for these conditions. To do this would have required the identification of a control group and, ideally, the random allocation of appropriate patients into telemedicine (intervention) and standard practice (control) groups.

We are therefore only able to describe the processes of care and satisfaction of patients for those recruited to the service, without being able to compare these to other similar patients for whom this service was not available.

The generalisability of our findings is also limited by the one site at which the link was set up with the main hospital, and the limited number of participating GPs and consultants. Although our in-depth interviews are revealing in terms of the views expressed by the clinicians participating in this pilot, practitioners at other sites may not share these views.

4.3 Implications of findings

The findings of this local evaluation are encouraging. The video link was shown to be feasible to run, and performed reliably across the sessions carried out during the evaluation period. Patients and GPs were, in the main, very pleased with the new service, and a considerable proportion of patients were able to be referred for day case surgery direct from the teleconsultation, bypassing the need for a further appointment at the outpatient clinic of the main hospital, situated some miles away from the area of the study. However, to assess the full impact of the service, as identified in previous research, an adequately powered randomised controlled trial would be needed, comparing the processes and outcomes of care for patients which were appropriate and offering the new service to others who were receiving standard care.

In addition, in terms of resources, the teleconsultation requires the presence of two doctors – the GP with the patient and the consultant at the other end. Whilst there may be benefits for patients – and perhaps the GP in terms of educational opportunity – this is an additional cost to the NHS against which the benefits need to be weighed.

5. Conclusions

The telemedicine link between the GP's surgery and the orthopaedic department of the district general hospital was found in this evaluation to bring benefits to patients through avoidance of travel to the hospital for outpatient appointments, and through high levels of satisfaction with the teleconsultation. The service worked reliably and the processes of care for patients and staff ran smoothly. The service was highly popular with the GPs and consultant who undertook the pilot, who all saw further potential for the service.

Before its widespread adoption could be recommended several questions remain to be answered that are outside the scope of this small-scale evaluation:

- What is the level of demand that exists in primary care for the service?
- How many practices would need to refer patients, and how sustainable would the service be with the current criteria for referral?
- What are the costs and benefits of the service in comparison to conventional care?

6. References

1. Melcer, T., et al., *A retrospective evaluation of the development of a telemedicine network in a military setting.* Mil Med, 2002. **167**(6): 510–5.
2. Melcer, T., et al., *A prospective evaluation of ENT telemedicine in remote military populations seeking specialty care.* Telemed J E Health, 2002. **8**(3): 301–11.
3. Pitt, K., *Prehospital selection of patients for thrombolysis by paramedics.* Emergency Medicine Journal, 2002. **19**(3): 260–3.
4. Terkelsen, C.J., et al., *Telemedicine used for remote prehospital diagnosing in patients suspected of acute myocardial infarction.* J Intern Med, 2002. **252**(5): 412–20.
5. Nordal, E.J., et al., *A comparative study of teleconsultations versus face-to-face consultations.* J Telemed Telecare, 2001. **7**(5): 257–65.
6. Wallace, P., et al., *Joint teleconsultations (virtual outreach) versus standard outpatient appointments for patients referred by their general practitioner for a specialist opinion: a randomised trial.* Lancet, 2002. **359**(9322): 1961–8.

Appendix II: Answers to Case Study Questions

Chapter 1

1.1: Evaluation of fruit stalls in four schools in South Wales

We could have done a pilot study. We could have introduced the stall in one school and asked children if they would like to use it. We could have got opinions on fruit stalls from children, parents and teachers and tried it out in one school to see how it worked.

1.2: Patient's self-evaluation after 4–12 weeks following propofol or xenon anaesthesias: a comparison

The two types of anaesthesia were comparable for effect but injected anaesthesia controlled post-operative pain better than gas and did not have the side effect of increased hunger/thirst. Therefore, injected anaesthesia was preferable to gas.

1.3: Evaluation of a community-based exercise programme for elderly Korean immigrants

This study examined a new exercise programme. This is not part of routine care and there are no national guidelines that Korean immigrants should be provided with an exercise programme. This is a new idea that is being investigated. Audit looks at the delivery of routine care to see if it follows national guidelines.

Chapter 2

2.1: The evaluation of family planning services in a mother-and-child centre

Why is the evaluation being done? What have other studies suggested are important in a family planning centre? What is the set up of the centre, are women referred, do they need an appointment?

2.2: Medical errors in an internal medicine department: evaluation of a computerised prescription system

This is a pretty good background considering it needs to be concise for an abstract. We might have liked a background more focused on the computerised physician order entry (CPOE), as it is not very clear what this is. How many errors are attributable to the ordering? How much difference will it make if we can reduce ordering errors?

Chapter 3

3.1: Evaluation of an occupational health intervention programme on whole-body vibration in fork-lift truck drivers: a controlled trial

If we were going to do a process evaluation we would look at why it worked in some places and not in others. We would look at how the programme was implemented in different areas, perhaps company policy towards WBV, attitudes of drivers to WBV, number of attendees at the programme, reasons for drop-out and opinions of the programme among drivers and company personnel.

3.2: Improving respiratory infection control practices in family physicians' offices

This evaluation looked at *how* training was delivered, by collecting activity logs and narrative reports. It examined if nurses where happy with the training they delivered (was it delivered well?), how many visits were made, aspects that contributed to success such as the Tool Kit and consensus building with office staff. It examined if GPs were happy with the visits. However, it did not look at outcomes such as whether respiratory infection control practices changed, it did not see if the intervention worked, it just looked at how it was delivered.

3.3: The burden of ankylosing spondylitis and the cost-effectiveness of treatment with infliximab (Remicade)

The cost-effective evaluation is looking at costs associated with the disease, such as loss of earnings through time off work or early retirement, the need to invest in items like stair lifts as a result of the arthritis, the loss of earnings to unpaid carers, the medical costs incurred due to the illness. These are set against the benefits of treatment which might reduce such costs as loss of earning and might give benefits measures in quality adjusted life years (years with less pain, improved function and time with a good quality of life). The cost of each year of good quality of life (less pain, less disability, capacity to have a normal working and home and social life) is put at £10,000 per year if people are treated with this drug on a long-term basis.

3.4: Evaluation of training needs within the community

The people who did not respond could have been quite happy with the training and didn't feel there were any needs to identify. The responders were likely to be the ones who were unhappy and wanted to tell someone that their training needs were not being taken seriously. Therefore, the evaluation suggests a very negative view of training (lack of time and money), but this could be a biased view from only getting the opinion of the people who are most unhappy with the situation.

The people who did not respond could be the managers. So we might be getting only the views of the front-line direct care staff – who have a poor view of managers. We might not be getting the managers' point of view about training.

Chapter 4

4.1: A nurse-led rapid access chest pain clinic – experience from the first three years

This is an outcomes evaluation. The abstract describes the process (what happens in the clinic) but the results reported are about the outcome of the clinic, and what the result was for patients. Therefore, this is an outcome evaluation.

4.2: Emergency pre-hospital treatment of suspected acute myocardial infarction patients, adjusted for focus

This is an audit. It is comparing what is done with the best care guidelines. Audits do not need ethical approval, so this does not need ethical approval.

Chapter 5

5.1: Time to insulin therapy and incidence of hypoglycaemia in patients with latent autoimmune diabetes in adults

This study needs ethical approval because we are examining records for research aims (not for the clinical care of these individual patients). Due to data protection we need approval to look at people's medical records if we are not their doctor.

Chapter 6

6.1: More is not better in the early care of acute myocardial infarction: a prospective cohort analysis of administrative databases

The hospital admissions data for the whole country were examined. Patients were classified as either attending a hospital without catheterisation facilities or with catheterisation facilities. Researchers examined the death rate and re-hospitalisation rate in both types of hospital. They showed that the rates of death and re-hospitalisation were no different for patients attending a hospital without catheterisation facilities compared to one with catheterisation facilities. However, the cost of catheterisation was double that in a non-catheterisation hospital.

6.2: The Bath ankylosing spondylitis patient global score (BAS-G)

The researchers just say they did a pilot study to develop the questionnaire, but do not give any details or information. They do not say if they interviewed patients or did a questionnaire, and they also do not say how many patients were involved. They do not state if it was patients who participated in the pilot study, or health care practitioners. They give no detail of how they developed the BAS-G.

The researchers validated the questionnaire on 392 patients. However, again they do not really say how they did this. We are given the results but are not been told very much about the methods.

Chapter 7

7.1: The REACT study: randomised evaluation of assertive community treatment in North London

The difference in the sample between the two groups (assertive vs. continuation care) was 7.14. So in the study assertive care gave more satisfaction.

But the 95 per cent confidence interval shows that in the population the difference might be as little as 0.9 (so very little difference between the two methods of delivering care) and as much as 13.4 (a large difference).

However, the lower part of the 95 per cent confidence interval does not cross 0 (that is, does not show any difference at all). So we would conclude in the population that assertive care would be better than continuation care.

To make our estimate more accurate we would need a larger sample size.

7.2: A pilot study for an emergency department-based organ donor card centre

The problem with doing seven separate tests is that a p value of 0.05 means the chance that we are wrong is 5 per cent. Therefore, if we do 20 tests we would expect five in 100 (which is one in 20) to be significant by chance. If we do seven tests, then there is an increased chance that one will be significant by chance.

One way to correct for doing multiple tests is to do Bonferroni's correction (www.childrens-mercy.org/stats/ask/bonferroni.asp). To do this we times the p value we get by the number of tests we do.

So, for example, in **A pilot study for and emergency department organ card centre**, the authors found that the likelihood being a current donor was affected by age and race ($p = 0.049$, 0.001 respectively).

0.049 times by 7 (number of tests) = 0.34 – a p value of 0.34 is not significant.
0.001 times by 7 (number of tests) = 0.007 – a p value of 0.007 is significant.
Therefore, the only factor which affects the likelihood of being a donor is race.

The principle of p values is that a test that results in a p value of 0.05 (five in 100 chance of error) means that the more tests we do the higher the likelihood we will accept the findings in error. For example, if we do 20 tests in our study (all the factors associated with interventions), we would expect by chance alone that one of these would have a p value of $p = 0.05$. This is a significant p value but has occurred simply by chance. This means we should try to do as few tests as possible.

Chapter 10

10.1: Evaluation of a one-day mental health course

We would like to know the type of people who did not return the 3-month questionnaire. Perhaps all the people who did not complete the question-naire would have shown that the course did not improve knowledge or confidence. Perhaps they did not return the questionnaire because they found the course a waste of time and so they could not be bothered to return it.

Glossary

Action research: Action research includes two fundamental aspects: (1) a commitment to change something, and (2) to work together as a team in collaborating to co-learn about a problem and the best solution. Action research follows a systematic scientific process of defining the question, defining the methods, then collecting and analysing data to feed into service improvement, on an ongoing, cyclical basis.

Advisory and steering groups: Advisory or steering groups are formed to guide, support and give advice to projects, they meet at key points during the life of the project and oversee the running of the whole project. There should be people from a mixture of disciplines, such as patient representatives, medical practitioners, researchers, and managers who are all able to contribute and advise on differ aspects of the project.

Aims and objectives: The aim is a general statement of what you want to do in broad terms. Objectives are more specific statements of how we will achieve our aim – the questions we will answer within our overall evaluation question. Our objectives should add up to no more and no less than our overall aim.

Bias: A systematic problem with the study. For example, the people who respond to a questionnaire might be different from those who don't (non-responder bias), and this means our results will be wrong. The interviewer might also have strong views to start with and suggest these views to the respondent (interviewer bias), influencing the findings of the study.

Case mix: Case mix describes the overall profile of patients attended or treated, in terms of condition or injury type and severity. Comparisons between places or providers of treatment need to be adjusted for case mix so that false conclusions are not drawn, based on outcomes, that are actually due to the type or severity of condition of patients treated rather than due to the quality of care provided.

Clinical effectiveness: This is about making sure that optimal care is provided – that treatment is given based on evidence that it works, and that local delivery of care is continuously assessed and improved.

Conflict of interest: Competing professional or personal interests that can make it difficult for a person to undertake the study impartially, for example where a person has shares in a drug company and then does a study to see if a drug is effective. Even if there is no evidence of improper actions, a conflict of interest can mean that others don't trust the findings of the evaluation. All conflicts of interest need to be declared in reports of findings.

Database: A structured collection of records or data. The database (place where records are held) can be queried and so specific records can be selected and taken out. For example, records of all the abstracts from articles published in journals are held in electronic databases on the Internet (such as MEDLINE), and they can be queried to identify specific papers of interest. Alternatively, we can put all the data we collect from questionnaires on a database and then select records or combine records to view the data in different ways.

Focus group: A group interview, made up of 8–10 participants, with a facilitator and note-taker. A structured or semi-structured topic guide is followed, to allow participants to respond to questions or issues and to discuss their views with one another as well as with the interviewer (facilitator). Sessions are taped and transcribed and analysed qualitatively.

Opportunity cost: This describes what you could have done instead of the service you are assessing, with the same resources. If we decide to invest in new drugs for people with heart disease, this means we cannot invest in new drugs for people with cancer.

Participatory methods: This is an approach where a range of stakeholders is involved in all the decision-making aspects of an evaluation. This might include patients or the people using and delivering the service – basically anyone affected by the programme or service should be involved in the decision-making processes of the evaluation. This includes developing the aims and objectives, deciding the design and methods, interpreting the findings and collecting the data as well.

Randomised controlled trial: A study design in which participants are randomly allocated to treatment groups – all participants have an equal chance of receiving the new intervention (that is being evaluated) or 'treatment as usual'/placebo. If randomisation is done properly, and the groups are large enough, people in each group will be similar in all aspects other than the treatment, allowing us to draw conclusions that any measured differences in outcome are due to the treatment, not differences in the case mix or other characteristics of the patients between groups.

References: Books, journal articles and policy documents that are referred to in the project write-up should be referenced so that the reader can find the original paper for their own interest. Full details should be given of the source document, which should be linked (by number or name and date) to the details, which should in turn be sufficient for readers to access the document.

Sample: The people (or places/items) we wish to include in our study, selected to be representative of the whole population (group) that we hope our findings will be applicable to.

Stakeholders: Someone with an interest in or who is affected by the evaluation, the people affected by the treatment (patients), and the people delivering the treatment (health professionals and hospital managers). Basically, people with a stake in the evaluation.

Standard deviation: A term which describes the spread of data around their average. The standard deviation is frequently used and reported when carrying out statistical analysis. It gives a good indication of how widely the data vary around the middle values.

Systematic review: Randomised controlled trials related to a particular question are identified systematically, and methods used to identify studies are reported in full. The results of randomised controlled trials are combined, through meta-analysis, sometimes allowing questions to be answered when individual studies were too small to definitively resolve them.

Index